from WAH LEE *to* CHEW KEEN

THE STORY OF A PIONEER CHINESE FAMILY IN NORTH CARIBOO

Liping Wong Yip

FriesenPress

Suite 300 - 990 Fort St
Victoria, BC, V8V 3K2
Canada

www.friesenpress.com

ISBN
978-1-4602-9429-1 (Hardcover)
978-1-4602-9430-7 (Paperback)
978-1-4602-9431-4 (eBook)

1. BIOGRAPHY & AUTOBIOGRAPHY, PERSONAL MEMOIRS

Distributed to the trade by The Ingram Book Company

When drinking water, remember its source.

- A Chinese idiom

CONTENTS

ACKNOWLEDGMENTS

Writing this book was not a solitary project. Along the way, I received support and inspiration from my family and friends.

To begin, I would like to express my heartfelt gratitude to Aunt Beatrice Keen Wong. Her kindness and unfailing support helped me better understand the Keen family and its history. A personal thank you to Donna Hong who embraced my early drafts of the story with enthusiasm. My thanks also go to members of the Keen family who shared their personal memories and family photographs.

I wish to thank my friend, Lily Chow, for her keen interest and research in Canadian-Chinese history, which has been a great source of inspiration. Many thanks to my writing group, the Wonderful Women of Words: Cathy, Faye, Fran, Gail, Janice and Sandra for their encouragement in my pursuit of this project. I would like to thank Lorna Townsend who generously shared her research findings. Special thanks to my friend, Alicia Thornton, who spent countless hours to proofread my manuscript and provide feedback with a good sense of humour.

A warm thanks goes to my brothers: Yimin Huang who volunteered to be my chauffeur and photographer in China; and Shengmin Huang who, to show his high regards for this project, helped finance the publication of this book so that it could be shared with a larger audience.

I would like to acknowledge the museums, libraries and archives dedicated to preserving historical documents and artifacts about B.C.'s past for future reference and research. Among them, my hat goes off to the Quesnel Museum, Barkerville Library, B.C. Archives and Library and Archives of Canada.

Last but not least, my gratitude and love goes out to my husband, Byron, and my two daughters, Julianne and Jennifer, who are a continuous source of strength and motivation.

PREFACE

What was supposed to be a side trip to take a picture of Grandpa Keen's village turned into a four-year quest to discover the history of a family. But looking back, my interest in Chinese-Canadian immigrants was sparked by personal encounters long before this journey into the past.

When I first arrived from Mainland China in the early 1980s, Roy Yip, the president of the Chinese Benevolent Association in Prince George, B.C., asked me to translate a letter from Chinese to English. Roy was a second generation Canadian-born Chinese, who could speak Cantonese but could not read or write Chinese.

Part of the association's work was looking after the welfare of the elderly Chinese residents in Prince George. For reasons I did not understand at the time, these retired Chinese were single males, who immigrated to Canada in the early 1900s as labourers and lived out their life without the company of any family members. On their passing, the association would take care of their estate and notify next of kin in China.

Roy's letter was from a family in China, relatives of a recently deceased Chinese man in Prince George. To his surprise, the deceased man was not single, as he had originally thought, but married with two wives and an adult daughter in his home village. In the letter, the wives expressed their wish to have their husband's body shipped back to China for burial.

This letter struck me as curious. It left me with questions about the life of the overseas Chinese, which I had understood to be a shameful part of Chinese history. I felt further perplexed when a parent in a weekend Chinese class demanded that his child not be taught simplified Chinese character writing, which reduced the number of strokes in many of the traditional characters. In his view, it was part of communist education and propaganda.

The truth is, writing with simplified Chinese characters began long before the Chinese communist movement, but it was strongly promoted by the government of the People's Republic of China. I was taught the simplified Chinese writing system in school. The parent's strong feelings compelled me to re-examine the recent history of China in a different light.

Growing up in Mainland China from the 1950s to 1970s, I was aware that families with relations in Hong Kong or overseas were deemed untrustworthy. The worst thing was to be pinned with the label "spy"; it blocked your career opportunities and any chances for promotion. Many families tried to conceal their ties with overseas relatives. As a young child, I learned to hide the fact that an uncle of mine worked in Hong Kong as a sausage maker because I did not want to be blacklisted by the school revolutionary committee.

However, decades of isolationist policies in China only increased my curiosity about the world outside its borders. When the door to the West opened, I came to Canada to pursue a western education and later made it my home. After thirty years living in Canada, I am beginning to understand some issues facing Chinese immigrants—maintaining trans-Pacific family ties, preserving cultural heritage and assimilating into a new society. The search for our family's roots motivated me and provided the opportunity to gain a different perspective on the history of the overseas Chinese.

Much of the information in this book comes from history books, newspapers, government censuses, immigration registrations, personal letters, unpublished memoirs and interviews. Of course, my focus was on the events that affected the Keen family on both continents and that helped me to connect the dots.

There were many twists and turns along the way but, in the end, I found many surprising discoveries laid out like gold glistening in a stream bed.

To avoid language confusion, I have used Cantonese or Sze Yup dialect pronunciation for names and places, with additional Chinese characters for clarification. For historical context, both metric and imperial measurement systems are used in accordance with the era involved.

Knowing our family's past helps us understand who we are today. The lives once lived were real and true. Thousands of Chinese immigrants travelled through the Cariboo since the gold rush era; to this day, the Keens remain the only Chinese pioneer family that stays in the region. They still live and work in their beloved town, Quesnel, over the last one hundred fifty years.

I realize that all past events are open to interpretation; this is my personal journey into the past.

The Fraser River Valley. (Drawing by Julianne Yip)

PROLOGUE

One hundred fifty years ago, on the old Cariboo Wagon Trail, a typical Chinese gentleman with a long braided pigtail was among thousands of Chinese gold seekers making the long trek to British Columbia's northern interior. According to Keen family lore, his name was Wah Lee. He was the first family member to leave his wife and family behind in search of fortune in Gum San, the "Gold Mountain."

Wah Lee first arrived at Port Victoria on Vancouver Island. From there, he found his way to Quesnel. There's no record of his first job, but later he acquired land in the town located in the blocks between Carson and Bowron Avenues. His first business venture was a general merchandising store called the Wah Lee Company. It catered mainly to the Chinese miners, with stock such as Chinese groceries, herbs, tobacco and clothing. He also helped Chinese miners write letters home.

In 1895, thirty-five years after Wah Lee's arrival in Canada, another young Chinese man also passed through the same port of entry in Victoria. After disembarking, he proceeded to the Canadian Immigration Registration Office and waited for his turn to be interviewed. He noticed that the immigration officer asked each newly arrived Chinese immigrant questions and scribbled on the pages in an oversized book. Perhaps the officer had a Chinese interpreter on hand to assist him.

When it was his turn, the officer wrote down a serial number, 19049, in the second-last column on the page. He glanced at the young man and asked, "Name?"

"*Chew Lai Kin* (周礼坚)," the man answered in his native dialect.

The officer penned "Chu Lai Kin" in the name column. He continued filling the next few columns. Port of arrival: Victoria, B.C. Date of registration: January 10, 1895. Certificate number: 14492. Age: 21. Fee paid: $50.

"Village?"

"*Tim Gum* (田金)," said the young man. The officer wrote down "Tim Kong." Well, close enough.

"District?"

"*Sun Wui* (新会)." The officer wrote down "Sun Woy."

He looked up and stared at the young man's face for a while then filled in the last column. Physical Marks or Peculiarities: "5 ft. 3in. - pigment in forehead; pigment in right-corner of mouth; pigment on both cheeks."

The young man was our Grandpa Keen who came to join his father Wah Lee in North Cariboo of British Columbia.

ONE
GRANDPA KEEN'S MAP

The first time I formally met the Keen family was at my wedding. It was 1984 in Prince George, B.C. New in Canada and not a member of the Christian faith, I opted for a house wedding. After our marriage was officiated at my parents-in-law's house, we proceeded to the Chinese tea ceremony.

According to Southern Chinese tradition, the tea ceremony is an important part of the wedding and a formal introduction to the families. The newlyweds are expected to serve tea to the elders of both families, beginning with the head of each family. In return, the elders give the newlyweds a small gift such as gold, jade jewellery or *lai see,* lucky money wrapped in a red envelope.

The tea served at the ceremony is not everyday tea. It is a special mix of regular tealeaves and dried lily bulbs, dried red dates, peanuts and lotus seeds. The extra ingredients are not added for medicinal purposes but for their symbolic importance. Each item is chosen for its expression of good luck and good wishes for the newlyweds.

Lily bulbs (百合 *bock hubb*) represent one hundred years of union. Both dried red dates (红枣 *hong joe*) and peanuts (花生 *far sung*) express the swift arrival of children. And lotus seeds (莲子 *lien gee*) symbolize good luck in bearing sons one after another.

Before the tea ceremony, my mother-in-law, Kay, asked me if I would mind serving the first set of tea to her parents. I agreed with pleasure but told her I did not know the protocol. I grew up in Mainland China where the old traditions and custom were condemned and banished into history. At that moment, an elderly Chinese woman, who had been invited by Kay to help with the tea ceremony, came forward and took my hand, leading my husband and me to the dining room.

A Chinese crowd is well known for its noise. This gathering was no exception. In the hallway, I could hear bursts of hearty laughter and loud conversation in English and Chinese. The guests were chatting to each other while waiting for the start of the tea ceremony. As we entered the room, the noise suddenly subsided and all eyes turned to us.

With the dining table removed, my parents-in-law and all the uncles and aunts were able to sit along both sides of the rectangular room, leaving a walkway to the mantelpiece at the far end. I kept my composure, staring straight ahead towards the end of the room. The mantel, which under ordinary circumstances would have been crowded with family photos and snapshots, had been cleared to make room for one eight-by-ten black-and-white photograph, a studio portrait of an elderly Chinese couple in North American attire.

The gentleman with a contented smile sat next to his beautiful wife who looked much younger than he. An exquisite broach and carefully crimped hair expressed her fashion consciousness. In front of the picture frame, two tiny Chinese wine cups were neatly arranged alongside two pairs of chopsticks.

As we approached the mantel, my husband whispered in my ear, "They're Grandpa and Granny Keen. Mom's parents." Before I could say anything, the Chinese woman handed my husband a cup of ready-made tea. He placed the cup in front of the picture next to one of the wine cups. I followed suit. We stepped back together and bowed three times to the picture.

Then we served tea to the rest of the family. There were so many uncles and aunts I had to address during the tea ceremony, most of whom I was meeting for the first time. I could not remember who was who, never mind which side of the family they belonged to. Everyone was either Uncle So-and-So or Auntie So-and-So and no one was introduced by his or her last name.

Thankfully, the Chinese woman who handed me each teacup murmured the guest's name in my ear. Most of the time, I politely mimicked what she said, remembering for one second and forgetting the next. It was not that I did not take the ceremony seriously. Her English was mixed with a very heavy Chinese dialect I was not familiar with. It took me many years before I could tell who belonged to which family, the Yips, the Keens, the Wongs or the Dongs. I did not even attempt to rank them according to their seniority in age as the Chinese usually did.

Soon after the wedding, my husband and I moved to Calgary, Alberta. The only time we could renew acquaintances was at family gatherings for special occasions, which often took place in a busy, noisy Chinese restaurant.

I did not pay much attention to the family names until I saw the Keen family tree compiled by Uncle Ken. I noticed that the Keen family name in Chinese was 周, pronounced as *Chew* in Sze Yup dialect. I asked my mother-in-law about it.

"Yes, Chew is my family name in Chinese. Somehow my dad got his name changed when he came to Canada. But that was a long time ago." She made it sound as if this name change happened centuries ago, too long ago to be any of her concern.

I did not dwell too much on the matter until I started looking after Kay, ten years before she passed away. During those years, I had the privilege of getting to know the Keen family better.

A hand-drawn map

After her husband passed away in 2006, Kay decided to move from Prince George to the Vancouver area. I helped her with the move to a one-bedroom apartment in a seniors' residence in Richmond, B.C. Kay gave up most of her possessions she had accumulated over eighty years, but she wanted to take her family photo albums with her. There were so many that she could only choose a few.

In her new apartment, she displayed a varied selection of old and new, large and small photos—a picture of her late husband, a portrait of herself before she got married, and some snapshots of her family, her children and grandchildren on different occasions. One photograph I could not help admiring every time I visited Kay was an old oversized family portrait taken in a photo studio in Vancouver.

The brown hues on the paper did not diminish the picture; instead they added a special effect. The picture captured the perfect moment for everyone—the relaxed elderly couple, the young adult faces, and the fashion of the time. Perhaps I was so mesmerized by the beauty of the photograph that I forgot to ask Kay what special occasion it was.

There were a few other old pictures that Kay kept in her dresser. During our visit, she would like to take them out and share stories with me about her growing up in Quesnel and Vancouver.

"We were so young and silly. I spent a lot of time with the Hoy girls," she would recall. "There are ten girls in the Hoy's family, don't you know? After my sister got married, I hung around with the older Hoy girls until I moved to Vancouver."

At the time, I had no idea who the Hoy girls were and assumed they were her childhood friends. One time when I took Kay out for a ride in Vancouver, we drove by Jericho Beach. At the mention of the beach name, she perked up: "My girlfriend and I used to work around here during the wartime. We sometimes met Chinese servicemen here after work." She grinned at the memory.

Once Kay casually mentioned that her father had another wife in China. "As you know, that was the old-fashioned Chinese way, when men could have more than one wife." She would brush away any further questions. Not wanting to be nosy, I changed the subject.

It was only after Kay passed away in January 2011 that I began asking her older sister, Beatrice, about the Keen family's history. While cleaning up the basement of my in-law's house in Prince George, I came across a pile of old newspaper clippings and black-and-white family photographs. Many of the people in the pictures were uncles or aunties I had met or heard of, but some I did not recognize at all. The charming smiles on their young, beautiful faces beckoned: "Come with us! We're having a great time."

One picture taken in the 1920s caught my attention. A gang of little boys and girls had lined up for a picture in front of an old wooden house. Who were these people? These old, forgotten photos triggered my curiosity about the Keen family history and I began to wonder where they came from.

On a visit to Vancouver, I had dinner with Auntie Bea and her family in a Chinese restaurant. During our casual conversation, I asked her: "By any chance, did your father tell you which village he came from?"

"No, I don't know the name in Chinese," Auntie Bea replied in a soft-spoken voice. "But I have a map to the village. My father drew the map and gave it to me when I got married."

A map? A map to a village in China! I straightened up in my chair and leaned across the table. "What year?"

"September 28, 1938." Auntie Bea announced the date clearly as if it were yesterday. "Dad told me if I would like to go home to China for a visit one day, I could simply follow the map."

I began counting on my fingers: "1938, 48, 58 ... 2008 and 2011 ... Auntie Bea, that was nearly seventy-three years ago!"

"Yes, that's about right. I never got the chance to use the map."

"Do you still have it?"

"Yes, I put it away in a safe place, but it's all in Chinese writing," she warned. "The map lists the names of stations of some sort. I remember my Mom saying that she and Dad used to go to a big market for groceries not far from the village. She said something about taking a train. I guess they took a train to go into town."

At that moment, my mind flooded with the possibility of finding the village. I could not contain myself.

"Auntie Bea, may I see the map?"

"Of course! You know Chinese and would understand what was written. But I doubt anyone is still living there."

"It doesn't matter. At least I could go take a picture of the village. I will show it to you when I return."

"That sounds like a promise." Auntie Bea grinned. Before the end of our dinner conversation, she suggested Cousin Connie might have some information about the village. "She went to China with her parents years ago."

Shortly afterwards, I received a photocopy of the map in the mail from Auntie Bea.

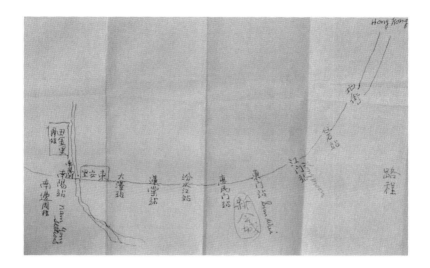

Grandpa Keen's hand-drawn map, 1938.
(Courtesy of the family)

The curved line on the hand-drawn map represented a route that started with the words "Hong Kong" in English on the upper right corner. It was followed by a series of Chinese words that were names of stations. Nothing indicated, however, if they were bus stations or train stations. Grandpa Keen had simply labelled it 路程 (Route) on the right-hand side. On the left-hand side, he had drawn two squares around the names of two villages 東安里 (Dong Oin Lei) and 田金里周姓 (Tim Gum Lei, Chew clan).

Interestingly, Grandpa Keen wrote all the names in the old Chinese style in vertical order from top to bottom except the one for Dong Oin Lei, which was horizontal from right to left. Along with the map, Auntie Bea sent me a photocopy of the envelope that held the map. The header "Wah Lee & Co. Est. 1870" was printed on the left corner.

The map arrived just in time, for I was preparing for my annual home visit to my elderly father in Canton, China. I also contacted Cousin Connie in Coquitlam and tried to get as much information as possible before my departure. Connie was very kind and gave me all she had—a business card of a relative named Zhou Wen Li.

"It's been a while since my last visit. I think she is my father's grandniece. The phone number on the card could be out of date because she was in the middle of a move when Dad and I met her." I was aware of the family relations in Hong Kong, but a little bit surprised to learn that the family had relatives living in China.

In May 2011, I found myself on a plane to China with a photocopy of the hand-drawn map and an out-dated business card in my hand. I had embarked on a journey that would send me back and forth across the Pacific Ocean to traverse over one hundred fifty years of family history.

Needle in a haystack

"Are you Zhou Wen Li?" I asked in Cantonese, holding the phone receiver very close to my ear, pinning all my hopes on the other end.

I felt like I was looking for a needle in a haystack. The only clue on the out-dated business card was Zhou Wen Li's name and her job position, a teacher in a technology institute in my hometown, Canton, the provincial capital city of Kwangtung.

I grew up in the city of Canton all my life before moving to Canada in the 1980s. Since then, there were so many developments that I felt like a stranger in my own hometown. Many old buildings were torn down and new roads built. Canton had grown into the largest city in Southern China with a population of 13 million in the city proper.

What worried me most about my search was the increasing mobility of the Chinese people. Unlike my time living there, when people were confined to one place and one job for life,

Chinese people nowadays were able to change jobs and move to new residences. So I asked for help from a long-time local resident, my oldest brother. He was a retired chemical engineer who used to work in the field of science and technology in the city.

The name of the institute rang a bell. My brother pulled out his cell phone and began searching for a number. "A high school friend of mine used to work in the same institute as a mathematics professor, but now he's retired. It won't hurt to ask him if he knows anyone by the name of Zhou Wen Li who worked at the institute faculty," he explained while dialling.

After talking to his friend on the other end, he handed me the phone. The retired professor handled my enquiry as if solving an algebraic equation, eliminating the irrelevant factors to find the possible answer.

"I think one person may match who you're looking for. Just give me a few minutes, I'll call you back." He hung up. A few minutes later, he called back and soon I was on the phone again, asking for Zhou Wen Li.

"Yes, I'm Zhou Wen Li." The female voice sounded coming from a great distance.

My heart stopped for a second. The speaker on the other end spoke Cantonese with a heavy Mandarin accent. I expected to hear Sze Yup dialect, a Cantonese tongue and dialect from Grandpa Keen's village. I switched to Mandarin, which I had not spoken for a while.

"My name is Liping. I'm a relative of Uncle Harry's in Canada. Do you know Uncle Harry?" My tongue felt caught between English and my awkward Mandarin. Uncle Harry was Auntie Bea's younger brother, but I did not know what the relationship was between Zhou Wen Li and Uncle Harry, so I kept the term "Uncle Harry" in English.

"Un-co-le Hae-rry? Un-co-le what?–" There was a pause at the end of the question.

"Uncle Harry from *jia-na-da*, Ca-na-da," I emphasized.

"From *jia-na-da*? Oh! Yes, yes! I know Uncle Harry. He's my great-uncle!" The excitement in her voice grew. At that moment, I realized I had found the right person.

It took only thirty minutes to conclude my search for a single person in a city of 13 million people. I felt a great sense of relief and accomplishment.

"My husband is a nephew of Uncle Harry. I'm so glad to get a hold of you. I got your contact information from Uncle Harry's daughter, Connie. I think you've met her."

"Oh, yes, a few years ago. Is Uncle Harry in Canton with you?"

"No, I'm not with Uncle Harry. He passed away in 2009."

"Oh, sorry. I didn't know." There was silence.

"Connie told me you were in the middle of a move during her last visit."

"Yes, I was moving to a new apartment and didn't have the new contact information yet. I'm very sorry about Uncle Harry. What did you say? Are you his daughter-in-law?"

"No, I'm Auntie Kay's daughter-in-law. Do you know Auntie Kay? She is Uncle Harry's sister." I could hear my own voice getting louder as I attempted to explain the complicated relationship in Chinese. I did not know how much Zhou Wen Li knew about her relatives in Canada. I heard a pause on the other side and changed the subject. "I happen to be here visiting my own family in Canton, so I tried to see if I could contact you."

"I'm glad you did. I've lost touch with Uncle Harry and Connie since I moved to my new apartment."

We turned our attention to arranging a convenient time to meet. I told her about my promise to Auntie Bea to find the village and take a picture of it.

"Have you been there before?" Zhou Wen Li asked.

"No, never, but I have a map Grandpa Keen drew. I thought I could just follow the map to get there." I told her the story of the map and my simple plan to find the village. "Have you been there?"

"Yes, many times. Only lately I've been too busy to go. It's not easy to find from the road, you know. Would you mind my joining you?"

"It'd be nice if you could come along with us," I said, laughing with relief. "I forgot to mention that Uncle Harry's granddaughter, Holly, is coming with us, too."

Holly was studying Mandarin in Shanghai out of a desire to connect with her Chinese roots. Before I left Canada, we had planned to meet in Canton and journey to the village together.

"Who? Hol ... Con ... Connie? Do you mean Connie is here with you?" Zhou Wen Li asked.

"Oh no, it's not Connie, but Hol-ly. She's Frances' daughter."

"Whose daughter?"

"Frances'. Do you know Connie's older sister, Frances?"

"Frances? I don't think I've met her."

"Never mind. Holly is coming in a few days and we're going to the village."

By now we were on the phone for over twenty minutes. I realized that the more I explained, the more muddled the translation sounded from English to Chinese and vice versa. One phone conversation was not enough to resolve the confusion so we set a date to visit the village.

I was about to hang up the phone when Zhou Wen Li suddenly added, "Oh, I forget to tell you. There is Ah Poh ('an old granny') still living in the village. I will inform her about our visit."

"What? Who is Ah Poh?" Nobody in Canada had mentioned any living relatives in the village.

"She is the only one from the older generation still living in the old house. We will visit her." Zhou Wen Li sounded surprised by my ignorance.

"Of course. We should visit her." I put down the phone, still reeling from this new piece of information. The conversation with Zhou Wen Li had put an unexpected spin on my original plan. Instead of taking a picture of the village, I was going to visit a living relative of Grandpa Keen's in his ancestral home!

A ghost railway

Early on the morning of June 4, 2011, one week after my phone conversation, I met Zhou Wen Li in a restaurant for a morning dim sum breakfast, a Cantonese tradition. Holly Benson, Uncle Harry's granddaughter, was there with us. She had flown in from Shanghai the day before. After breakfast, we piled into my brother's car. We were heading for Grandpa Keen's home village—Dong Oin Lei.

We could not follow Grandpa Keen's map to get to his village. Before my trip to China, I had found out that the names depicted on the map were train stations of a railway that no longer existed. Few in present-day China were aware of the railway; for those who did remember, their memories of the railroad were vague. In my school days in China, no word of the railway was mentioned in the history textbooks. It became an esoteric subject that historians would take up for their academic theses.

The ghost railway was called Sunning Railway (新宁铁路). "Sunning" (新宁) used to be the name for Toi-san County (台山) until 1914. It was one of the three Chinese railways funded and built with private Chinese capital, much of it from overseas Chinese in the United States, Canada and Southeast Asia. The initiator and fundraiser for the railway was a man from Toi-san County named Chin Gee Hee (陈宜禧). Up to the beginning of the twentieth century, boats and sampans were the primary source of transportation in the Pearl River Delta. Chin saw the economic benefit of a railway in the region.

Chin went to the United States in the mid-nineteenth century to work as a labourer, first in a gold mine and then in the Pacific Railway construction. Later, he became a merchant and labour contractor in Seattle and supplied workers and crews for railway and highway construction. As a leading, successful overseas Chinese entrepreneur, Chin returned to China in 1904 and lobbied the Qing government to let him build a railroad in the Sze Yup (四邑) region in the Pearl River Delta.

After Chin raised $2.7 million and was granted the charter from the Qing Court, construction of the first section began in Toi-san County in 1906; it opened for service in 1909. By 1911, the second section from Toi-san to Sun-wui was operational, and in 1913 the rail reached the port of Kongmoon (江门) in Sun-wui. At the end of 1920, its western line from Toi-san to Hoi-ping was completed. The length of the railway stretched to one hundred thirty-three kilometers and crossed three counties.

Powered by steam locomotive, the locals called the train "fire vehicle". It could carry hundreds of passengers and tons of freight at the same time. If China did not become embroiled in wars, the railway could have reached its economic potential. Unfortunately, it was dismantled at the beginning of the Second Sino-Japanese War in 1938. Today, only small remnants of the rails can be seen under the paved country road.

Older generations of Chinese Canadians are familiar with the Cantonese term Sze Yup (四邑) because most early Chinese immigrants came from that area. In Cantonese, Sze means "four" while Yup means "county." The four counties are Sun-wui (新会), Toi-san (台山), Hoi-ping (开平) and Yin-ping (恩平). Among these counties, Sun-wui is the only one that maintains its ancient name and it's the county where the Keen family came from.

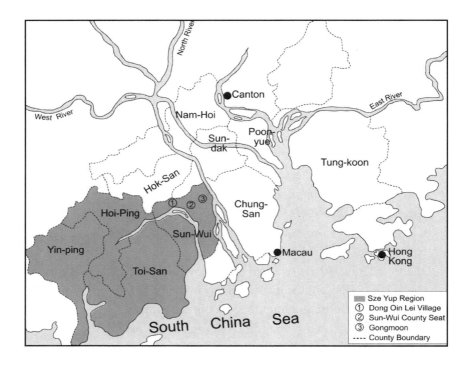

Map of Sze Yup region in the Pearl River Delta.

Sometimes, the early Chinese immigrants preferred to say they were from Canton rather than from a specific county. The term Canton was much easier to understand for westerners. They used to call Kwangtung province, Canton, a Portuguese transliteration of Kwangtung. Today, Canton is often referred to as the capital city of Kwangtung province.

Located in the southwest of the Pearl River Delta, the Sze Yup region is heavily crisscrossed by a network of rivers and streams, especially in Sun-wui County where the Tam River (潭江) flows through before emptying into the South China Sea. The four counties are so intertwined that people in the region share many similar traditions and custom and speak a similar dialect called Sze Yup dialect. Linguistically, the dialect is a part of the Cantonese language system. The majority of people are Han Chinese who originated from the northern plains of China. In the Keen family, Sze Yup blood runs deep. Apart from Grandpa and Granny Keen, who came from Sun-wui County, several of his in-laws came from the other three counties.

Today's Sun-wui County covers an area of 1,387 square kilometres, half the size of Greater Vancouver, with a population of 740,000. Blessed by a subtropical climate and fertile land, Sun-wui is the rice bowl of the Sze Yup region. Besides rice production, the county has a long history of growing citrus fruits, particularly mandarins. The world-renowned dried mandarin peels come from this area and have been used in traditional Chinese medicine and cooking for hundreds of years. Sun-wui is also nicknamed the County of Fountain Palms (葵鄉), not just for the plants that grow there but also for its famed palm leaf handicrafts which have been created for centuries.

Grandpa Keen's village, Dong Oin Lei or 'east peace village' (東安里), is one of a hundred villages under the administration of Da Zap Township or 'big marshland' (大泽镇) in Sun-wui County. A thousand years ago, the area was a marshland north of the Tam River, which gradually turned into an alluvial plain suitable for farming. Villages were built and a market town was formed. Over the years, the names and boundaries of the four counties have changed for reasons only the government knows. But Sze Yup is a place thousands of overseas Chinese call home.

A web of relations

Dong Oin Lei is about one hundred kilometers as the crow flies from Canton. In my childhood memories, it used to take a whole day by boat or bus to get to any destination in the Pearl River Delta. In 2011, our car travelled on a new four-lane highway at a speed of one hundred twenty kilometres per hour. In less than one hour we would reach the village. Sitting at the back seat of the car, Zhou Wen Li, Holly and I tried to figure out how we were related to each other and to the old granny we were about to visit.

"Who is this Ah Poh in the village?" I asked Zhou Wen Li.

"She's a ninety-year-old granny, a daughter-in-law of Wife No. 2, I think. She's the only family member still living in the old house. Her husband died a long time ago."

"How do you address her?" I knew Ah Poh was a common term for granny in Cantonese, not a correct salutation for an elder relative.

"*Sook-poh* (叔婆)."

"Oh..." I paused to think it through, as the salutation meant the wife of a great-uncle. Zhou Wen Li was three generations younger than Ah Poh, in the same generation as Holly.

I could find no equivalent term in English to reflect the proper kin relationship for Holly, who grew up in Canada and learned the English way. In Chinese kinship, there are specific salutations to designate relations that are "internal" and "external," or "paternal" and "maternal," as well as the hierarchy of relationship according to generations. For anyone not familiar with the pecking order in Chinese society, it could be hard to follow. I settled on a simplified term of "great-aunt" for Ah Poh in relation to Holly.

In a fast moving car, I found it difficult to untangle the relationship amongst the three of us. I began with what I knew by explaining the name of Zhou Wen Li. "Zhou" is Grandpa Keen's original family name in Mandarin as "Chew" in Sze Yup dialect. "Wen Li" is a given name. The Chinese written form Zhou Wen Li (周文丽) is in the proper Chinese name order—family name followed by given name.

From Zhou Wen Li, I discovered Grandpa Keen did not have two wives, but three. Zhou Wen Li's family belonged to Wife No. 1 and Holly's to Wife No. 3. And we were on our way to visit the family of Wife No. 2.

Feeling like I was being ambushed constantly by new information, I tried to keep calm and figure out how Zhou Wen Li and Holly were related in English terms. With four generations of involvement from different wives, I could not explain it without a diagram. Zhou Wen Li offered a pen and note pad.

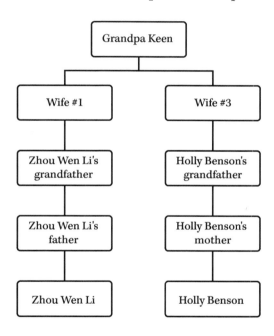

The diagram clearly explained that the grandfathers of Zhou Wen Li and Holly were half-brothers. Their parents were first cousins. That made Zhou Wen Li and Holly second cousins, at least according to western culture. Both Holly and Zhou Wen Li were satisfied with my explanation. However, I refused to put myself in the equation because I was related to the family through marriage. Adding on only complicated the existing confusion.

On the way to the village, we paid a short visit to a legendary Wong clan temple twenty kilometres north of Dong Oin Lei. Wong was my maiden name and the clan temple was located in the same county as the Keen's. My brother, who was our volunteer driver, wanted to pay homage. After the temple visit, we stopped for lunch at a roadside eatery advertising its special dish *bah zam guy* 'steamed chicken' (白切鸡), a favourite dish among the southern Chinese and the Keen family.

This side trip took us off the main highway and confused our guide Zhou Wen Li, who was used to travelling by a more direct route. Thankfully, a villager from the Wong clan kindly pointed us to a backcountry road, a shortcut to Dong Oin Lei. To make sure we understood, he drew the directions on a piece of paper ripped from a brown paper bag. Following the new map, we took the one-lane road cutting through farmland.

It was only the beginning of June, but the temperature soared to thirty-eight degrees Celsius. A white blazing sun hung above us in the hazy sky. The air outside the car was thick and humid. Inside the car, the air conditioning blasted at full force. There was no traffic on this country road except for our car. With the fan blowing and the car motor humming, Zhou Wen Li and Holly drifted off.

My mind was too busy to rest. The landscape outside my window was peaceful and beautiful. Green rice paddies stretched for miles on both sides of the road. Gently rounded hills in the distance were covered with shrubs and eucalyptus trees. An electrical power line ran parallel along one side of the road. Sometimes a cell phone tower rose from the middle of a rice field. Judging from the small clusters of houses here or there, there were not many big village settlements on this side of the land. I wondered why Grandpa Keen would have left this beautiful countryside.

Before long, our car followed a curve leading to a paved street that was lined with old buildings at least three storeys high. Their European design looked quite out of place in the middle of a rural countryside. Had we not seen the sign, Da Zap Township Government Administration, we might have thought we were lost in a strange land.

Da Zap was one of the train station names on Grandpa Keen's map. It must have been the market town that Granny Keen did her grocery shopping many years ago. She later told her daughter Beatrice about taking a train to the market when living in China. Unexpectedly, the back road took us through the town's main street.

"Stop the car, please!" I called out. I wanted to get out and take a look, perhaps feel it.

The buildings were old and weathered, each obviously modelled after the western style —grand Roman-style pillars, yellow paint with white trim, arched frames and projecting balconies. Because of limited space, the narrow buildings often shared walls with next-door neighbours. The ground floor was reserved for shops or stores while the upper floors were family living quarters.

To gain more living space, the second floors jutted out over the sidewalk and were supported by pillars forming an arcade for pedestrians. This style was very popular in the commercial districts in the city of Canton.

Buildings with arcade in Dah Zap old market town, 2011.
(Photo by author)

A hundred years ago, on market day, the street would have been bustling with vendors selling homemade food, vegetables, fruit, pork, chickens, fish, livestock and daily goods. On special occasions, a Cantonese opera would be invited to perform on a makeshift stage. Nowadays, the bustling market crowd had moved to the new section close to the new highway, leaving most of the old buildings vacant or neglected. Only one barbershop was open; a couple of old folks sat around chatting.

The backcountry road through Da Zap market town was a pleasant surprise, better than planned. I wished I could take a stroll down the main street, but my travel companions reminded me of Ah Poh, who was waiting for us in Grandpa Keen's village.

First visit to Dong Oin Lei

The village was tucked away from the main road. If Zhou Wen Li had not been with us, we would probably have missed it. Off the main road, a short dirt path led us to an embankment along

Tim Gum Creek. With overgrown tall grasses on one side and a running creek on the other, our car slowed to a crawl.

At the end of the dirt path, we came to a fishpond on the right and an open area on the left. A lonely tilting watchtower stood by the edge of the pond, guarding a cluster of grey brick houses on its right. There was no village gate or a sign to mark the entrance. Our car veered to the left, following a cement strip toward a wide-open space that stood between the houses and another fishpond. The strip served as an open yard for thrashing and drying crops as well as a common place, where villagers met and chat at the end of a hard-working day while their children played. When we arrived, it was in the middle of a hot day; everyone stayed indoors.

We parked under a banyan tree by the edge of the fishpond facing the village. Stepping out of the car, I could feel the heat waves radiating from the baked ground. The calm surface of the water and the luscious green bamboo bushes across the pond cast a cooling effect. Conveniently located by the bank of Tim Gum Creek, Dong Oin Lei had a few fishponds. Water ran freely from one pond to another, then off to irrigate surrounding rice paddies.

Fishponds were integral part of the rural landscape in the Pearl River Delta. Every rural settlement used to have at least one in front of its village. In the past, the pond served as a catch basin for household wastewater that provided nutrients for the fish. Once in a while, fishponds would be drained for fish harvest and a thick layer of rich mud at the bottom would be scooped up as organic fertiliser for crops. This land-water ecosystem used to be popular in the Delta. Today, this practice was vanishing due to the increase of urbanization and industrial farming.

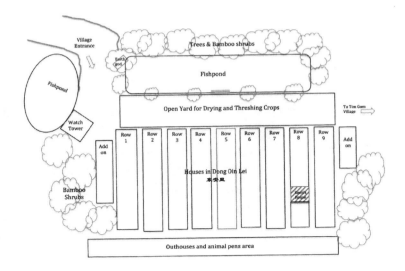

Layout of Dong Oin Lei Village.

Looking toward the village, there was not a soul in sight except for a middle-aged woman who appeared from a gap between the houses. Wearing a white sun hat, she looked towards us with a broad smile on her tanned face. Zhou Wen Li gave her a wave.

"She's Ah Poh's daughter-in-law," Zhou Wen Li said as we walking toward her, "She moved back from Hong Kong to take care of Ah Poh."

Ah Poh's daughter-in-law did not introduce herself but kept smiling. "I'm happy you're all here. It's a very hot day. Quick, let's go into the house." Swiftly, she led the way in the front.

The village was laid out in a typical pattern for the Sze Yup region. Houses were built in rows and each row had several houses, often with adjoining walls. The gap between each row was called *hong* 'lane' (巷), and the entrance to the house usually faced the lane. Perhaps this tight-fitting style was a way to maximize the space in an area that suffered from farmland shortage.

There were at least nine rows in Dong Oin Lei, and each row had at least nine houses. The lane between the rows was just wide enough to let a bicycle through. Walking in single file, we entered Lane Eight.

Lane Eight where Grandpa Keen's house is located, 2011.
(Photo by author)

All the houses were built with slate-blue bricks. Over the years, the blue colour had turned to light grey; some were even covered with lush moss. When made of solid bricks, the walls could go up to fifteen-feet high with small windows in the upper part of the walls—there were very few windows at eye level.

Brick houses cost so much to build in the old days that mud houses were more common in rural areas; most of the houses in Tim Gum village were built this way. It was not the case in Dong Oin Lei. The entire village was built with slate-blue bricks from the ground up, a display of wealth. Obviously, the villagers must have had money in the past.

We passed by many houses with rusting padlocks that appeared unoccupied. Some were clearly abandoned with crumbling walls and collapsed roofs; others had vegetation hanging down from tiled roofs. Ah Poh's daughter-in-law explained in an apologetic tone, "These houses are old, perhaps over a hundred years old. Only a few old folks still live in them. Many have moved away to live elsewhere."

Apparently, the majority of villagers had moved out. Many of them lived in places such as Hong Kong, Malaysia, Australia, or North America. The houses they left behind became ancestral sites that they returned to for visits. A few houses had red paper strips glued above the doorway, an indication of ownership. Down the lane, our hostess stopped by an entrance flanked by two bright red Chinese New Year couplets. She turned to us and said, "Here we are. This is our home." Above the doorway, a small blue house plate read No. 6 - No. 7, Lane Eight, Dong Oin Lei (東安村八巷 6 – 7 号).

By the entranceway stood a silver-haired granny with a big smile on her wrinkled, tanned face. Ah Poh, in a loose fitting blue striped blouse and flowery patterned pants, had been waiting for us since she woke up that morning.

"Come in. Make yourself at home," Ah Poh said, inviting us into her home. One by one, we entered the house through a foyer and proceeded to the family hall where Ah Poh had laid out some plastic stools for our visit.

The inside of the house looked different from what I had expected. Instead of a house with three rooms (family hall and two bedrooms) and two kitchen porches, Grandpa Keen's house had a family hall flanked by two bedrooms on each side, a kitchen porch and a foyer. It was a big house that occupied the space of two small houses.

As is the custom, more than one family would share a house such as between families of two brothers or two wives. The kitchen porch on each side of the house served as each family's entrance. The family hall always served as a common area with a side open to an outdoor courtyard. In Grandpa Keen's house, the courtyard was partially covered and a wall sectioned off the family hall from the courtyard. All the walls were whitewashed; only the floor had the original terracotta tiles.

There was not much furniture besides a long wooden bench, a worn-out wicker chair, a few chairs and a couple of portable tables tucked away at the far end of the room. An old television sat on top of the Earth god altar while a white refrigerator stood beside a bedroom door, looking a bit out of place.

On the back wall a ladder leaned against a small loft where the family ancestral shrine was placed. In other regions in Southern China, the altar for ancestral shrine was usually on the ground floor. But in the Sze Yup region, the shrine was placed high up in the loft, from where, the family believed, the ancestral blessing could reach those who were far away over the oceans.

Everyone sat down around a low-rise table. Ah Poh sat on a wicker chair beside a bedroom door. I sat next to her on the long wooden bench. She still could not believe her relatives from Canada were actually visiting her.

"*A-ya, ya-ya,* finally people from Canada come home to visit us, *ho-loh, ho-loh, ho* ..." Her trembling voice sounded as if she was chanting a sad tune. Her head tilted backward with her eyes closed. Then, she turned to me.

"What did you say? You're a granddaughter of Gou Shong (高祥)?"

"No, but I'm–" I struggled to find the proper term to explain, "Ah ... my husband is Gou Shong's grandson."

"Oh, yup." She gave a nod. "You know Gou Shong is my father-in-law's name, don't you?"

I smiled. Throughout our visit, Ah Poh addressed Grandpa Keen by his name, Gou Shong, not Chew Keen, or Keen.

Ah Poh continued. "I'm a daughter-in-law of Gou Shong's second wife. Lung Shong (龙骧) was my husband."

"What's your maiden name?" I asked.

"Yu, Yu Liu (余料)," said Ah Poh's daughter-in-law. She handed me a cup of tea. Ah Poh looked up and smiled. She leaned towards me.

"I have three children, two sons and a daughter. My husband is gone a long time ago, so are my two sons. My daughter lives in Hong Kong. She's married with four children." Ah Poh sounded as if she thought Hong Kong was a special place to live. Pointing to her daughter-in-law, who was busy passing around tea and food, she continued. "She is my eldest son's wife and lives in Hong Kong, too. She came back to take care of me. I'm getting old. Guess, how old I am?" She did not wait for my answer but continued with pride, "Ninety-six. Actual age."

I smiled in return. Elderly Chinese usually had a nominal age that was reckoned at birth as one year and then another year was added after the Chinese New Year. Therefore, actual age could be two years younger than nominal age. Ah Poh could be ninety-eight years old in nominal age.

"Come, help yourself." Ah Poh pointed with a bony finger to the food on the table. "Try the sticky rice. It's homemade."

It happened to be the time of the year for the Dragon Boat Festival. Sticky rice wrapped in bamboo leaves was a special food for the festival. Fresh lychee, a tropical fruit, was also in season. I was in disbelief that we were gathering in the family hall of Grandpa Keen's house, chatting and sharing homemade food.

But soon I realized our conversation was getting lost in translation. Four languages were being spoken simultaneously—Sze Yup dialect, Cantonese, Mandarin and English. Zhou Wen Li could speak Mandarin and Cantonese. Holly only knew English and some Mandarin. Our hostesses, Ah Poh and her daughter-in-law, only spoke Sze Yup dialect and very little Cantonese. I was the only one who could juggle the four languages at the same time. The attempt was exhausting and slow.

I was glad when Ah Poh's granddaughter, Zee Lan, and her husband came in. The young couple took time off from their factory work to meet us. They could speak Sze Yup dialect as well as fluent Cantonese and Mandarin, which they had learned in school. As they picked up the conversation with Zhou Wen Li and Holly, I was left alone with Ah Poh.

Despite her advanced age, Ah Poh was able to recall the Chinese names of all Grandpa Keen's children in Canada as if she knew them personally, but she preferred to call them by numbers. Beatrice was *Yee Gu,* 'No. 2 girl' (二姑), and Kay was *Sam Gu,* 'No. 3 girl' (三姑).

"So, who is your mother-in-law?" she asked me. When I told her Kay's Chinese name, she picked up on it right away. "Oh, that's Sam Gu. Is she still here?"

I told her of Kay's passing and Ah Poh was silent for a moment.

"She must have been very close to her nineties. Ninety is a long life," she said. "What about Yee Gu? How is she doing?"

"She is doing well." My mind was busy working on the numbering. If there were No. 2 and No. 3 girls, there must be a Da Gu 'No. 1 girl' (大姑). "What about Da Gu?" I asked. "What's her name?"

"Oh, Da Gu, her name is Kin Bao (琼宝). She was my husband's sister. She married to Malaya." She made it sound like the girl was given away to the country of Malaysia. She elaborated no further about her husband or children. When the conversation turned to Grandpa Keen, Ah Poh held up three fingers.

"Three. Gou Shong (Grandpa Keen) had three wives. My mother-in-law was the second wife. The first wife died during the Japanese war." Then she changed the subject to the war, "Oh, that was a terrible time. We all fled from the village. There was nothing to eat. The first wife starved to death later, poor soul."

She paused, the wrinkles on her face gathered in grief. Each wrinkle could tell its own story. She told me how they escaped from the raid of Japanese soldiers and hid in the graveyard. She closed her eyes, shaking her head as if trying to shake off the bad memory. She opened her eyes again. "It was a terrible, terrible time. I don't know how I survived it."

"Did you meet your father-in-law?" I asked, changing the subject.

"Oh no," she moaned. "I never met him in person. When he and his third wife were in Hong Kong, only my mother-in-law, oldest son and daughter went to see them. My husband and I couldn't go." She wiped away some tears with her fingers. "Oh, it is sad. I missed the chance to meet him. Very sad."

"Have you seen him in pictures?"

"Oh yes, only in pictures." At that moment, her daughter-in-law who had been listening the entire time got up from her chair and went into one of the bedrooms. She came out with two charcoal drawings of Grandpa Keen and his second wife. They must have been done in Hong Kong during his visit.

As I examined the charcoal paintings, Ah Poh asked me, "Do you really come from Gum San?"

"Gum San? No, from Canada."

"Yes, I know. The folks here call Canada Gum San (Gold Mountain). Gou Shong's father was one of the first men from the village to go to Gum San." She lowered her voice as if telling me a secret: "You see, Gou Shong's father used to be a tofu maker before he left here. Later, he sent for his son, Gou Shong."

"Was Gou Shong his only son?"

"No. Gou Shong had an older brother, but he died a long time ago. His wife remarried and left their two children, a boy and a girl. The boy later went to Australia and the girl married a man from Malaya."

"Do you know when Gou Shong went to Gum San?"

"No, that's a long time ago. Before Gum San, he was a teacher in the village school."

Ah Poh had a wealth of information about the family. I wished we could stay longer, I had so many questions to ask, but we had to move on to the next visit. Holly wanted to go to Hoi-ping to visit a relative from her grandmother's side.

Perhaps I would have a chance for another visit on my next trip to China. I decided, the next time, I would be better prepared. Ah Poh looked healthy for her age. She even insisted on walking us to the car to see us off.

"Remember to come again." She patted my hand and bid us good-bye with a wave.

Letters to Grandpa Keen from China.
(Photo by author)

TWO
IN SEARCH OF WAH LEE

Actually I did keep my promise to take a picture of the village for Auntie Bea, but never did I expect to meet Grandpa Keen's relatives in the house where he grew up. The brief visit left me with more questions than answers.

As a newcomer to the Keen family, I was puzzled by the change of family name; the rest of the family, however, took it in stride. After the village visit, I realized I knew very little about the history of the family, apart from stories and anecdotes—nothing about our great-grandfather who was the Cariboo trailblazer.

When I asked what his name was, every family member in Canada unanimously agreed it was Wah Lee, although none had ever met him. Logically, if Grandpa Keen's name followed the English name order and was changed from Chew to Keen, why had "Lee" not become the last name of our great-grandfather? He was the first person in Canada. What were the Chinese characters for Wah Lee? The discrepancy in names intrigued me enough to begin my quest—to clarify the name of our great-grandfather, once and for all.

Who was Wah Lee?

In today's digital world, I was able to search on the Internet in the comfort of my own home. A cursory search turned up people named Wah Lee in far-flung places such as China, the United States and New Zealand. The one that matched my search criteria was listed in the "British Columbia City Directories" in the *First Victoria Directory 4th Issue* of 1871. Under the heading of Williams Creek, "Wa Lee" was first listed as a storekeeper in the Chinese section. After this initial listing in the directory, the name "Wa Lee" often appeared as a trader or shopkeeper in the Cariboo region of the B.C. Directories from 1871 to 1939.

According to the directory, Williams Creek was the early name for today's Barkerville, a historic town in British Columbia. During the gold rush of the 1860s, tens of thousands of gold seekers descended upon the area, including thousands of Chinese. Wah Lee must have been one of them. The gold rush is long gone, but the town of Barkerville remains as a historical heritage site from that era. It maintains a large collection of Chinese artifacts.

My phone call to the Barkerville library led to a dialogue with the museum librarian. With the librarian's help, I gathered some references—a photograph, some old newspaper clippings, the Assay Office Ledgers and legal documents. All were related to the name "Wa Lee". Conveniently, I was able to examine most of the information online except for legal papers stored in the B.C. Archive.

Barkerville main street, 1868. Photo by Frederick Dally.
(Courtesy of the Royal BC Museum and Archives: Image F-00305)

The photograph was taken from the north side of Barkerville town looking towards the south side. In the foreground on the left hand side is a store sign that reads "WA LEE WASHING & IRONING." Along the right edge of the sign there are three small Chinese characters 和利店 in the old Chinese script order running from top to bottom.

The anglicized Wa Lee matches the first two Chinese characters 和 利 in Sze Yup dialect, meaning, "to bind in harmony for benefit". The last character *dim* 店 means store. In this picture, Frederick Dally, a dentist and photographer, not only captured the early life of the gold town, but he left us solid evidence that Wa Lee was a laundry business in Barkerville as early as 1868, three years before British Columbia became a province.

Wa Lee laundry was not aware of this free publicity. There was no need for it since the laundry was located in the centre of town in the white miners' section. Other large Chinese merchandise companies such as Kwong Lee & Co. purchased regular advertisements in the local weekly English newspaper, *The Cariboo Sentinel*. Wa Lee was rarely mentioned in the newspaper, in fact only twice.

The first appearance was in September 1869 when Sir Anthony Musgrave, the newly appointed Governor of the United Colonies of Vancouver and British Columbia paid an official visit to Barkerville. Wa Lee joined six other prominent business firms to represent the Chinese residents of the Cariboo and welcome the new governor.

The second appearance was an announcement of the arrival of provision pack trains on June 12, 1875:

> *The Weather – We think we are safe in saying that summer has at last set in, that is so far as temperature is concerned. Heavy rains have fallen during the past few days, and the different creeks are very high. No damage by the freshet reported so far.*
>
> *The First Pack Trains of the season arrived at Van Winkle on Thursday. Guitlerres Bros. pack train, which left Yale on the 12th May, loaded with merchandise for Beady & Townsend; and Raphael Carancho's train loaded for Wa Lee & Co.*

The arrival of pack trains signalled the opening of the Cariboo Wagon Road, the only supply route to the gold mining town from the south. During winter, the Cariboo Wagon Road in the northern interior could be covered with a few feet of snow, making it impassable. Those who could not afford the journey down south before the winter had to manage their provisions very carefully until the pack trains arrived in spring.

In such a remote and isolated gold field, the announcement of a fresh load of supplies and provision was most welcoming news to any miners, white or Chinese. Obviously, Wa Lee & Co. not only catered to Chinese miners, but also served other miners. It's worth noting that Wa Lee's laundry business by then had grown into a merchandise company big enough to commission a pack train from the south.

As a major gold mining town, Barkerville had a government assay office on site that acted like a bank where miners could deposit their gold dust or nuggets. Over the years, the office had kept all the transactions on file. Amongst them were one hundred sixteen deposit ledgers in the name of Wa Lee from 1869 to 1896. The ledgers indicated that the depositor was a trading firm.

In these references, Wa Lee was a well-documented business name. It corroborated what the Barkerville Museum curator told me—that Wa Lee was a firm name for a group of people. In the curator's opinion, I was embarking on an impossible mission to find the real name of our great-grandfather. But I thought that behind the scenes of this firm – managing its everyday operations – there must be an individual or group of individuals. One of them must be our great-grandfather. I was determined to uncover his real name.

The name game

Who, then, were the owners or founders of the company? One source containing the names and details is the Canadian National Census, which dates back as early as 1825. The year I was interested in was 1881, when 4,383 Chinese immigrants were first included in the national census. With no proper given name on hand, I used the company name Wah Lee once again for the census search.

Two records with the spelling "Wha Lee" popped up on the computer screen. Regardless of different English spellings, the pronunciation for the Chinese characters is the same in Sze Yup dialect. Both records were registered in Quesnellemouth (today's Quesnel) with the same information – Name: Wha Lee; Nationality: Chinese; Occupation: Merchant; Residency: Household #15. The only difference was the age. One was sixty-one years old and the other, forty-seven years old.

Aware of the different spelling in anglicized Chinese names, I searched the 1891 national census. There was no Wah Lee in the Quesnel district. I found only one Wah Lee in the Richfield District (today's Barkerville), sixty miles east of Quesnel. This Wah Lee was a seventy-one-year-old general trader/storekeeper living with a thirty-one-year-old Chinese cook named Ah Foon, in a one-storey wooden rooming house. His age was consistent with the sixty-one-year-old Wha Lee in the 1881 census ten years earlier. This seventy-one-year-old Wah Lee could be our great-grandfather. But, I still believed it was not his real name.

The early census was more concerned with collecting demographic data rather than recording accurate personal names. After all, the census meant nothing to the Chinese immigrants since they did not intend to settle permanently in Canada. In comparison with many other Chinese records in the census, our great-grandfather was lucky enough to be identified with his Wah Lee business name. Most Chinese immigrants hardly left any trace behind. What remained were their anglicized names: Ah Foon, Ah Fun, Ah Him, Ah Sing or Ah Soot. These names posed more questions than answers. To make matters worse, the same name often appeared in many entries.

The word "Ah" in a Chinese name does not signify anything; rather, it serves as a diminutive affix used in front of a person's given name to express familiarity and kinship. Only the character following Ah is the person's name or nickname. But what were the Chinese characters for Foon or Fun or Him or Sing or Soot? Compounding the problem was the different dialects involved. Without a written form in Chinese, one sound could mean any number of different words or things.

In this case, the anglicized Sze Yup accent made it extremely difficult, if not impossible, to recover the original Chinese characters associated with the names. That is how many early Chinese immigrants lost their family names while their first names became their family names.

One reference I found helpful for Chinese name search was Dr. Ying-ying Chen's dissertation *In the Colonies of T'ang*. In her work, Dr. Chen focused her archaeological study on early Chinese communities in the North Cariboo region. In Table 46 of her dissertation, she compiled over a thousand Chinese names—1,366 to be exact—from the Chinese Hong-men account books and the Chinese Benevolent Association of Canada files, of people who lived in the North Cariboo region in the 1880s. But without knowing our great-grandfather's personal name, I could not even begin to refer to the list for help.

Realizing I was searching for the name of a person who no longer lived, headstones came to mind. In Chinese cemeteries in Canada, headstones were often inscribed with both English and Chinese names. When I proposed the question to a Barkerville curator, I was told that the Chinese community in Barkerville treated their dead according to traditional Chinese custom: the bones of those who died in a foreign land were laid to rest for a few years before their remains were exhumed and shipped back to their home villages for a final burial. Many empty graves left in the Richfield or Stanley cemeteries in the Barkerville area were evidence of such a practice.

By the time I had made all these connections in my research, it was the dead of winter. The name trail seemed to be growing cold. I had one more source—the old documents of Wah Lee

& Co. stored in the vault of the B.C. Archives. I could not wait until the spring when I could make a trip to Victoria, the capital of British Columbia. Some answers might lie in those old, dusty documents.

In the name of Wah Lee

In early spring of 2012, I flew from the foothills of the Rockies to Victoria on the west coast. All the spring flowers were in full bloom in the coastal city—cherry blossoms lined the streets with a dazzling array of colour.

I was ready to pick up the trail and navigate through the archives. A friendly staff member reminded me to put on a pair of white gloves before she handed me a box of files. I did not have to dig deep. Up in front was the first folder marked "Wah Lee & Company." Inside were three old affidavits titled "Declaration Partnership" dated in three separate years: 1899, 1907 and 1911.

Carefully unfolding the century-old documents, a piece of dried red wax fell out from one of the papers and dropped to the desk. At first glance, the 1899 document could have easily been mistaken for an assignment sheet of student homework if not for the official notary public seal. The piece of ruled paper looked as if it had been ripped from a paper pad. Its yellowish colour was evidence of time, but each blue ribbon of ink left by the typewriter remained as clear as if it had been typed the day before.

My excitement grew as I read the first line of the document. Four anglicized names of the original partners of Wah Lee & Co. had been inked onto the paper—Sin Cup, Yut Chow, Chew Chung and Chew Tut. Clearly, the original partnership of Wah Lee & Co. was formed on August 1, 1866; one year after the Cariboo Wagon Road reached the newly established gold town of Barkerville. The four partners claimed themselves to be merchants residing in Quesnel. Together, they carried on a trading and general merchandise business in both towns of Quesnel and Barkerville.

The affidavit was carried out on November 15, 1899. Two of the original partners, Chew Chung and Chew Tut were present and signed their names. Because Sin Cup was not present, a person called Chew Chu Joe was his representative and signed the affidavit. Curiously, in Yut Chow's signatory spot, there were three Chinese characters 日潮子 with English writing declaring "his mark." Yut Chow was the sound for the first two Chinese characters, 日潮, and the third character, 子, meaning son. Perhaps it meant the son of Yut Chow signed the document.

The content of the 1907 document was similar to that of the 1899 document, without any Chinese writing. There were additional handwritten English notes indicating that Sin Cup and Yut Chow had died in China and their shares had been passed down to their brothers and sons.

The 1911 document was a declaration for a different partnership, but under the same company name of Wah Lee. It stated that the original partnership of Wah Lee & Co. was dissolved and a new partnership of thirteen individuals was established on August 1, 1910. They formed three groups in three places—Barkerville, Quesnel and Hong Kong. In this document, some signatories put their name in both English and Chinese, others only in English. There were over a dozen signatories in all three documents.

Based on my research, Grandpa Keen was sponsored by his father to come to Canada and had been working with him in the Wah Lee store before taking over the company business. After examining the three documents on hand, I dismissed the 1911 document that contained no original partners of Wah Lee Company. I focused on the two earlier documents and tried to establish a father-son connection.

The handwritten notes in the 1907 document drew my attention. They stated that the company shares were passed down to their sons after the death of two original partners. One particular note struck a chord: "Yut Chow is now represented by his son Chute King." Grandpa Keen's anglicized name is Chew Keen; it was very close to the sound of Chute King. What's more, the 1901 national census indicated Grandpa Keen was in Canada working in the Wah Lee store while Yut Chow died in 1902 in China.

There was no doubt in my mind that Chute King was a variation of Chew Keen. That made Yut Chow (日潮) Chew Keen's father. I had done it! After being buried in the vault of the B.C. Archives for over a hundred years, the name of our great-grandfather was finally unearthed.

More than one Chinese name

As I celebrated finding our great-grandfather's personal name, I was informed that the Barkerville library had received a box of Keen family artifacts containing Chinese books and handwritten scrolls. Because most of the content was in Chinese, the librarian was not able to tell me what they were about.

Up to this point, my research had been hindered by the lack of information in Chinese. The words "Chinese handwritten scrolls" were good enough to lure me on the 1000 kilometre drive from Calgary to Barkerville to take a look in the box. Little did I know this trip would lead to yet another major discovery about the identity of our great-grandfather, Yut Chow.

The brown cardboard box marked "From the Keens" contained books such as a bible in Chinese, some Chinese calligraphy exercise books, a songbook in Chinese and some written paper scrolls wrapped in oversized brown envelopes. The paper scrolls were delicate and precariously thin. With great care, I gingerly removed them and unrolled them onto the big library worktable. My hands trembled with excitement when I saw handwritten Chinese characters in black ink. My heart burst with joy when I read the first two Chinese characters, Gou Shong (高祥). This was Grandpa Keen's other Chinese name and the letters were addressed to him.

The scrolls were personal letters to Grandpa Keen from Hong Kong, Australia and China from 1917 to 1928. There were over one hundred letters inscribed in Chinese ink on Chinese paper with vertical red lines. The script was written with a small brush pen in old Chinese calligraphy. The letters read from top to bottom and right to left. For reasons unknown, Grandpa Keen had carefully pasted the letters in a series, one page after another, perhaps, in the order he received them, so they could be rolled up in the old Chinese fashion. I felt like a gold prospector who had just discovered the mother lode.

I had no time to read what was written as I spent the rest of the day taking photographs of each letter, frame by frame. Back at home, it took me months to transcribe each letter from the old Chinese script to modern Chinese and then translate it into English. In traditional Chinese style, there was no punctuation or paragraph. This posed a great challenge since I had little training in old Chinese. Without any context, some words had ambiguous meanings. Moreover, the letters were not necessarily glued together in chronological order.

After countless hours of sorting and reorganizing, the contents of the letters finally came to light, revealing many untold stories of the village and Grandpa Keen's family in Dong Oin Lei. All the letters were addressed to Grandpa Keen except for one, a very short letter with a list for some Chinese dried goods. At first, I dismissed it as an insignificant grocery list. When I transcribed the content, however, I made an important discovery about the signature at the end of the letter.

The letter was addressed directly to Dah Seen, who regularly wrote to Grandpa Keen. Although the letter was addressed to

Dah Seen, as I will explain shortly, the contents were relevant to Grandpa Keen. The translation of the letter reads:

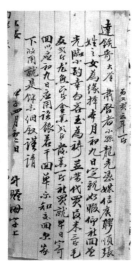

May 5, 1924

Dear Dah Seen,

With the help of a matchmaker, my grandson, Lung Gong, has been matched up with a girl from Choeng's family. May 12th of this month has been picked as the auspicious engagement date when betrothal gifts will be exchanged with the Choeng's family.

To prepare for the gifts, I would like to order three pounds of dried shrimps; two pounds of dried shiitake mushrooms; six pounds of dried squid; two pounds of dried lily bulbs and one pound of hair moss. It would be greatly appreciated if you could deliver them as soon as possible before May 9th. The payment will come out from the family expenditure account. Please keep the receipts.

Best regards,

Sing Chun Mou

P.S. Also one pound of cloud ears (wood fungus).

Sing Chun Mou's Letter.

(Photo by author)

The contents of this letter aside, what I found most revealing was the relationship amongst the people mentioned in the letter. Lung Gong is Grandpa Keen's oldest son. Although the letter was signed in the name of Lung Gong's grandmother, this name, "Sing Chun Mou", was not her name. The character "Mou" means elderly woman as well as wife; put together with "Sing Chun" signifies wife of Sing Chun. Therefore, Sing Chun is the name of the father to Grandpa Keen and the grandfather to Lung Gong.

Unexpectedly, I discovered another name for Yut Chow in a betrothal gift order. From the beginning, I complained about the lack of information written in Chinese. Now I had not only one Chinese name, but two: Yut Chow (日 潮) and Sing Chun (升 照).

With our great-grandfather's second name in hand, I returned to Dr. Ying-ying Chen's list of Chinese miners. I found him as Chew Sing Chun (周 升 爐) in a short list of twelve Chinese miners who came from Sun-wui, the same county as Grandpa Keen, and lived in Quesnel. Though the last character 爐 (Chun) looks very different from the other Chun (照), it sounds the same in Sze Yup dialect and is a matter of simplified and traditional Chinese writing.

Another clue is that the letter was not written by Sing Chun's wife, but a paid letter writer on her behalf. She was illiterate, just like the majority of Chinese women at the time. The letter writer might have written down the name by sound and created this discrepancy.

Nonetheless, traditional convention allowed a Chinese person to have more than one name, particularly a male. Besides his family name, he could have a given name, a courtesy name, a generation name, an assumed name, a nickname and so on. A man was addressed by his appropriate name in accordance with the occasion, which was especially important when he entered office or had a business. A female's name was not as important because she was not going to hold an office or work outside the home. Once she married, she belonged to someone else.

Over time, rules for names were relaxed and folks in rural areas kept two or three names for themselves— a surname (姓), a given name (名) and a courtesy name (字). The surname was passed down through the males of the family. The given name was bestowed by parents at birth and known within the family circle. The courtesy name was given when the person comes of age, say, in a wedding engagement. Perhaps, that's why our great-grandfather had two names Yut Chow and Sing Chun. The question is, which is his given name and which his courtesy name?

Looking at the names of Chinese miners in the short list, one thing struck me. Some names shared not only a family name but also a character within their names. That brought to my attention another name tradition called the generation name. This tradition has been all but forgotten in today's China. The example here illustrates six names from the list that also contains our great-grandfather's name.

Chinese Name	Family Name	Generation Name	Individual Character	Anglicized Name
周升爐	周	升	爐	Chew Sing Chun*
周升逞	周	升	逞	Chew Sing Tseng
周升操	周	升	操	Chew Sing Chua
周升揖	周	升	揖	Chew Sing Tsep
周升萱	周	升	萱	Chew Sing Xuen
周升翁	周	升	翁	Chew Sing Wown

According to the Chinese naming tradition, the character Sing (升) can be a generation name, which is prescribed by successive characters in a generation poem composed by a local scholar and approved by a committee of family elders. Each male born to the same generation in the same lineage will share the same character in his name regardless of his birth date or birth order. Sometimes, that could lead to a strange situation where a two-year-old baby boy from a preceding generation could be the uncle of a twenty-year-old nephew from a successive generation in the same lineage.

To identify each individual in the same generation, a different character, which I refer to as "individual character" in the list above, is added to the generation name. Thus, the combination of the generation name and the individual character form a courtesy name, which is then officially recorded in the lineage pedigree. The placement of the generation name in a courtesy name can be in either position as long as the convention is consistent throughout the same generation.

In regard to our great-grandfather, Yut Chow could be his given name (名) and Sing Chun his courtesy name (字). The people in the list sharing the generation name Sing (升) could be his brothers or cousins.

One source that would confirm my finding and parse out the relationship among the Chinese people in the list was the Chew lineage pedigree. I decided to pay a visit to Grandpa Keen's village, Dong Oin Lei, where the pedigree was kept.

Dong Oin Lei Village, 2013.
(Photo by author)

THREE
THE CHEW PEDIGREE

Once again I travelled back to Dong Oin Lei in October of 2013 during my annual visit to China. This time I came with a mission: to find the lineage pedigree, a genealogical record of the Chew clan. Traditionally, every lineage or clan keeps a copy of its own pedigree, which contains a record of all the names of male members born to the same lineage or clan in generation order. Sometimes a well-kept record can go back a dozen generations and span several hundred years.

The famous Confucius family in China has the best-kept genealogical record in China, if not the world, dating back over two thousand five hundred years and covering seventy-seven generations. Keeping such records is a component of ancestral veneration in Chinese culture based on the Confucian idea of filial piety, a virtue of respect for one's father, elders and ancestors.

Before the trip to the village, I was aware of the difficult task of finding the Chew lineage pedigree. During the Great Cultural Revolution from 1966 to 1976, thousands of lineage and clan pedigrees were destroyed in the inferno of Mao's Red Guards simply because they were part of the old Confucian regime and considered a threat to communist ideology.

Since the 1980s, as China marched towards greater urbanization, an urgent need to find one's ancestral roots became stronger among the Chinese people. Some clan pedigrees – including the Wong clan pedigree of my natal family – began to surface from the ashes. I believed that, if it had survived the wars and political campaigns, the Chew lineage pedigree would be kept in Dong Oin Lei. Our great-grandfather's name would be recorded in the pedigree as well as the names of those who went to Gum San with him.

Return to Dong Oin Lei

On the way to Dong Oin Lei, I stopped at a regional university in Kongmoon City and tried to get some help from the Overseas Chinese Research Center. This official approach would have worked if I had the time to wait, but my time was running out.

Ah Poh had since passed away. Shortly after our meeting, her health began to deteriorate and she died at the age of ninety-eight. Her daughter-in-law returned to Hong Kong so no one was living in Grandpa Keen's old house. With my brother volunteering as chauffeur, I decided to go straight to Dong Oin Lei and ask the villagers directly. I recognized my efforts might not amount to anything, but it was worth a try.

When we got to Dong Oin Lei, it was in late afternoon. The sun barely peeked out from behind thick grey clouds. At the far end of the grain ground, a patch of golden rice was thinly laid out. A farmer was attending to his newly harvested crop with a wooden rake, turning and spreading the grains.

We parked the car by the village watchtower that I had regarded as an abandoned structure during my first visit. A couple of middle-aged women were milling about, paying no attention to us. I walked around the watchtower looking for an entrance. As I transcribed Grandpa Keen's correspondences, I had learned stories of the village. The watchtower was one of them.

Surrounded by rice paddies and fishponds, the watchtower was the tallest cement building in the area. Built with funds raised by the overseas Chinese in Canada and Australia, it was once an intended refuge for villagers from bandit attacks. It was designed like a fortress; each floor had a trap door and small portholes cut into the walls for rifles. From the top floor balcony, one could see the surrounding countryside as far as the hills to the north and the Tam River to the south. The original paint of the watchtower had faded away revealing the inky outlines of underlining decorations. The building looked as if it had been forgotten for some time, quietly waiting for someone to reclaim it.

A sad feeling arose inside me. Looking at the derelict tower, I felt an urge to apologize to those who had funded the construction of the watchtower with their hard-earned money.

"Do you see the holes?" A woman's voice interrupted my thoughts. "Those are gunshot holes from the Japanese machine guns."

I turned around and saw a woman standing behind me, her hand pointing upward. My eyes followed her hand and looked up. There were a dozen holes on the upper tower wall. If the woman had not said anything I would have mistaken the holes as evidence of a crumbling old building.

I acknowledged her with a smile and she smiled in return. I asked her in Cantonese if she knew anyone in the village who would keep a copy of the lineage pedigree. She looked at me, puzzled. I explained what a pedigree was. She kept shaking her head.

"I'm a woman. I don't know nothing." She smiled, covering her mouth with one hand. Then, a motorbike approached. She waved it down and pointed to a young man on the motorbike. "Ask him. He is the village bookkeeper. He knows everything."

"What do you want?" asked the young man in a heavy Sze Yup accent before I could introduce myself. He was in his late twenties or early thirties, short and slim with a deeply tanned face. He planted one of his feet on the ground to balance the motorbike as the engine continued to idle.

"I'm a relative of Chew Gou Shong and I'm looking for *Zuk Pou* 'lineage pedigree' (族谱)," I tried to explain in Cantonese. "You know, the record for the villagers."

"What?" The young man tilted his head towards me as if trying to catch what I was saying above the noise of the running motor.

"Zu-uk Pu-oo." I emphasized each syllable in a loud voice. "It's a book that has all the names from the Chew family." I spoke in an impromptu dialect, combining an imitated Sze Yup accent and distorted Cantonese. "Do you understand what Zuk P–"

"Yah, yah, I know what Zuk Pou is," he interrupted. He turned off the motor and parked the bike beside me. "Yes, I think there is such a record, but not in the village office. Only a few *lao mon* (elders) in the village keep copies at home."

"Could you find out who has a copy?"

"That, I don't know, but I could try. First, let me make some calls." He walked away a distance and began making calls on his cell phone.

I watched him scribble numbers on the ground with a broken piece of red brick. He finally looked at me and said, "Yes, a few elders keep copies, but you are not allowed to look at them."

"What? Why?" My voice was unusually loud and attracting onlookers coming home from the fields and nearby factories. They stopped and gathered around us, wondering what was going on.

"Just because ..." the young village bookkeeper hesitated, "... well, only the male descendants of the Chew clan are allowed to look at the book." His face flushed with embarrassment.

I thought I came with enough preparation. Never did I expect to encounter such patriarchal thinking in the twenty-first century!

Traditionally, only the male descendants were accounted for in the genealogical pedigree. As a general rule, female members were deemed insignificant and not recorded. The only trace of a girl's identity was her family name followed by the word Shee (氏), meaning "née" in English, or "born." But that was in the past.

Since the beginning of the last century, Chinese girls had their own names and kept them unchanged even after they got married. In my early school days, I used to be drilled by Mao's words: "Women hold up half of the sky." Men and women should be equal partners. I could not believe that women in the twenty-first century were still being treated inferior to men.

At the same time, I realized I was a lone woman in this fight and needed to keep calm. My opinion did not matter to them. Raising my voice would not get me anywhere. I changed tactics, lowering my voice and playing up my role as an overseas Chinese looking for family roots.

"As I told you, I came all the way from Canada for this."

"And ... and what did you say? I mean who are you? How are you related to Chew Gou Shong? I didn't get it the first time." The young bookkeeper collected himself and tried to take control of the situation. When I clarified my family relationship, he made some concessions.

"Why don't you bring his sons and grandsons back here with you? Then they could take a look at the book themselves."

What kind of suggestion was that? I stared at him in disbelief.

"Yes, I wish I could, but you see, even if they were here they don't know any Chinese." I managed to regain my composure as I tried to reason with the bookkeeper.

He just shrugged his shoulders. "I'm sorry, but I don't know what to do. I just follow the rules."

At that moment, I realized we were locked in a stalemate. Then from nowhere, a man riding on a motorbike that was bigger and more powerful than the bookkeeper's passed by. He stopped and parked outside the circle of onlookers.

The driver was a middle-aged stocky man with a broad but lightly tanned face. He looked older and was taller than the bookkeeper. He walked straight to the bookkeeper and talked to him with his back towards me. Then the two men walked away from the crowd in private consultation. A few minutes later, the bookkeeper returned to me and said in a conciliatory tone.

"I think my uncle might have a copy of the book, but ..." he looked up at the grey sky, "it's dark and my uncle is an old man in his nineties and doesn't live in the village. If you don't mind coming back, I would arrange a meeting for you to see him tomorrow."

It sounded like a final offer. Dark rain clouds had been gathering over the low sky during our discussion. The humidity in the air was thick and oppressive. It looked like a late summer rainstorm was in the making. The curious crowd had broken up and gone away. A yellow glow emanated from the small windows and a delicious smell of cooking wafted through the air. It was suppertime.

I looked around searching for my brother. He was on the sideline watching the events unfold without saying much. He did not understand Sze Yup dialect. But foremost, he was a Wong and not a member of the Chew clan. There was an implied understanding that no outsider or stranger should put his nose in the clan matter at all.

My brother came over to me and made a concession. "Well, it's late and we don't want to trouble the elder on such short notice. We'll come back tomorrow morning." With that, my brother and I took leave and decided to stay for the night in Kongmoon City where we could be close to the village.

The generation poem

The young bookkeeper kept his word and took us to see his ninety-two-year-old uncle the following day. During our introduction, I found out the relation between the elder and the bookkeeper was not as close as I had presumed. However, the bookkeeper called the elder "uncle" out of respect.

The elder introduced himself as Chew Dah Guk (周达濑). He was very glad to see me. After shaking my hand, he told me that his grandfather also went to Gum San (Gold Mountain), the one in Australia in the 1860s.

During the course of our visit, the elder confirmed that quite a few men from Tim Gum village went to Gum San at that time. Unfortunately his grandfather died in Australia before his father was old enough to join him. Later the bones of his grandfather were shipped back to the village for burial. While the elder was telling me his family story, he wrote down their names on a piece of paper to clarify their names and relationship.

The characters such as Sing (升) and Gou (高) captured my attention. Trying not to be presumptuous, I asked carefully, "Do the characters Sing and Gou in their names indicate that they belong to different generations?"

"Yes, but how do you know about that?" The elder looked up at me, surprised.

I continued. "I think there should be a generation poem to go with the names, right?"

"Yes, of course!" Without any hesitation, words began rolling off the elder's tongue as if he were reciting a famous Chinese poem:

可道承先德 (*hoi dou sing sin dak*) Blessed by our ancestors' virtues,

立维万世猶 (*lap wai mang sai yau*) Uphold them for generations to come,

升高达华岳 (*sing gou dah wah ngok*) Rise high to reach the highest mountains,

建业耀家邦 (*geen yip yiu gaa bong*) Bring honour to our homeland.

The ninety-two-year-old elder beamed with pride as the young bookkeeper sitting next to him looked on, puzzled and quiet.

"What's that all about? I never heard about a generation poem!" the bookkeeper finally said.

"You see, each word in the poem indicates a generation," the elder tried to explain.

"What words?" The bookkeeper looked more perplexed.

"Just a minute." The elder got up from the chair and went into his bedroom. He returned with an oversized book. He produced a loose paper from the book and showed it to us. A handwritten generation poem was carefully copied down on the piece of translucent paper.

"Do you see those three words at the beginning of the third line?" The elder pointed at the words. "SING-GOU-DAH 'rise-high-reach' (升-高-达). These three words represent three generations. Sing (升) is my grandfather's generation, Gou (高) my father's and Dah (达) is my generation."

"Your grandfather Gou Shong (高祥)," he turned to me, "is in the same generation as my father's Gou generation. And mine is in Dah generation."

"Then, what generation am I in?" The bookkeeper interrupted. "My name is Hong Leong (洪亮). It doesn't fall into any generation according to the poem." Only then did I learn that the bookkeeper's name was Chew Hong Leong (周洪亮).

"Hong Leong is your *manh*, 'given name' (名). You should have *zee*, 'a courtesy name' (字) with a generation character from the poem. Check with your old man," the elder suggested. "Don't worry, young people today know nothing of it," he said to comfort the bookkeeper.

Our conversation turned to the lineage pedigree. The elder showed me the oversized, self-bound booklet. The pedigree was not labelled; it was a photocopy of an old one. The cover was a ledger form used to protect the pedigree.

"This Zuk Pou 'pedigree' (族谱) needs a good update," the elder said. Then he took another piece of loose paper from the booklet that contained names and lines all over it. "I'm trying to put down as many names as I remember, but my eyesight fails me. It's not finished yet."

Flipping through the pages of the booklet, I found names of the lineage recorded neatly in the old Chinese fashion from top to bottom and right to left. There were a lot of generations recorded. Turning to the last few pages, I spotted twenty-two generations recorded.

"Do you know how to read it?" the elder asked. It was a legitimate question because the old style of Chinese books began from the right to left. I nodded.

"Even if you do," he warned, "you have to know which branch your family belongs to. You'll need more time to look into it."

He was right. A couple of hours visiting would not help me locate the names of Sing Chun or others, especially under the elder's watchful eyes. I took a short cut by showing the elder the list of names I had copied from Dr. Chen's dissertation before the trip.

"Yup, these men came from Tim Gum, our ancestral village," he said after taking a close look at the list. "There it is." His finger pointed at the name Chew Sing Chun (周升爐). "That's the name for Gou Shong's father."

I felt a rush of excitement inside but held it back as the elder continued.

"He belonged to the Sing generation just like my grandfather. Many from Sing generation and a few from Gou generation went to Gum San, some to Australia and others to Canada."

"Do you know Sing Chun's *mang* (given name)? It's something like Yut Chow," I asked.

"No, I don't. Only his family would know. Anyone outside the family would have called him by his courtesy name. Besides, they've been gone a long time ago. Nobody will know or remember." The elder was frank. Then, he went back to my list of names.

When he got to the last name on the list, he squinted as if looking at something blurry and trying to make it out.

"I think this word is supposed to be *Cup* (翕) not *Wown* (翁)." He grabbed a pen and wrote down the correct word beside Chew Sing Cup's Chinese name. I followed his strokes closely and realized they had a different combination of radical parts. This time it was not a matter of simplified or traditional Chinese. They were totally separate characters with different meanings.

"Sing Cup was from Kee Gong Li (奇岗里), another village not far from Tim Gum. They belong to the branch of our people because we share the same *bah kong* (ancestor)." The elder looked at the bookkeeper who nodded his head in agreement.

The day went by very fast. Soon, the elder's son returned home from work, signalling that it was the end of our visit. And yet, I did not have enough time to take a good look at the pedigree.

"It will take some time to find the family line in the book," the elder said to me. "Now that you know where the book is, you can come back for it next time." Obviously, the pedigree wasn't leaving his house.

After being granted permission, I took photos of the generation poem and the introduction of the pedigree. I said good-bye, feeling my mission was half accomplished.

On the one hand, the visit was fruitful. I had learned about the generation poem and confirmed our great-grandfather's courtesy name. I also found out that Sing Chun (Yut Chow) and Sing Cup, two of the original partners of Wah Lee & Co., were cousins. On the other hand, I did not have the pedigree. I was sure the book contained a lot of answers about the Keen family history.

Back in Canada, I found out I was not the only one interested in the history of Chinese miners in Quesnel. Lorna Townsend, the former chairperson for the Quesnel District Museum and Heritage Commission, was doing research for the family of Chew Sing Cup. We exchanged our research information and Lorna helped me locate the missing Wah Lee in the 1891 census. He was in the census, listed under the name Joe Sin Cott (Chew Sing Cup). He was fifty-eight years old and had a family, a wife and children, in Quesnel.

And so, the pieces of the puzzle started falling into place—the name of our great-grandfather, Wah Lee's partnership declarations and the generation poem. Only the Chew lineage pedigree was missing from the big picture. To me, the pedigree was the final piece of evidence that would confirm my findings.

Chew lineage pedigree

Knowing where the pedigree was, I could not let it go without looking at its contents. The records would go back to the beginning of the clan history and contain statistical information of each male member such as names, birthday, marriage status as well as offspring. Most important of all was the revelation of relationship to one another. In February 2015, two years after my last visit to the elder, I set out again for the Chew pedigree.

To ensure the success of my third visit, I contacted the village bookkeeper, Chew Hong Leong once I arrived in China. It happened to be the Chinese New Year. I forgot that everyone was busy during the holidays. When I got a hold of him, it was two days before my return trip to Canada. On the phone, he informed me that the elder had passed away shortly after our last visit and the copy of the pedigree had been passed down to his son.

With a sense of urgency, I met Chew Hong Leong in Dong Oin Lei the next day and went to visit the elder's son. For the third time, my brother was my chauffeur as well as a photographer. He brought along his powerful camera to take photos of the entire pedigree in case permission was granted.

The village of Dong Oin Lei looked different, somehow rejuvenated. The old narrow embankment path to the village had been widened and paved with cement. The old watchtower stood out above a newly poured cement square. The young bookkeeper was waiting by the tower, beaming with pride.

"What do you think of the village square?" he said looking at my brother instead of me, "Money from three levels of government. The village, the region and the province have helped improve the road and the village's appearance." He showed us around explaining their future plan. "We've decided to restore the watchtower as a landmark for the village. It's not finished yet."

I felt a sense of comfort that the old watchtower was finally reclaimed. It was still a reminder of the past, but no longer lonely and sad.

"I've found out my courtesy name," the bookkeeper told me with a big grin. "It is Chew Dah Hao (周达浩). I'm in the Dah generation." He turned out to be in the same generation as the elder he used to call uncle, even though they were nearly sixty years apart.

The elder's son was at home to welcome us and graciously allowed us to photograph the whole pedigree. Page by page, my brother focused and refocused the camera lens. He kept clicking away until the last page was photographed. When we said goodbye to our hosts, the bookkeeper reminded me that the records in the pedigree should not be shared with anyone outside the Chew clan. I agreed but wondered what the reason was behind the condition. It was not until I began studying the pedigree at home that I gained some understanding of the tradition.

Unlike church registries that keep meticulous records of each member's name, date of birth, marriage and death, the information provided in a Chinese lineage or clan pedigree is arbitrary and not standardised. In general, it contains three parts: the introduction, the records and the creed for the clan. It is usually handwritten, copied and kept by the elders responsible for maintaining and updating the records.

The introduction contains clan history, its origin and migration. It often traces the lineage to a common ancestor, usually accompanied by drawings of the ancestor and the location of his grave, which is related to Feng Shui belief.

The second part was the bulk of genealogical records of all male members in the lineage such as:

- Generation
- Names, including given names, courtesy names, style names and the like
- Dates of birth and death
- Burial location
- Surname and home village of wife or wives
- Burial location of wife or wives
- Names of children
- Names of adopted children
- Indication of any children dead before age twenty

The last part is the clan creed based on Confucian ideas. It sets the guidelines and codes of conduct for its members. Any member who acted against the codes, such as elder abuse, incest, banditry, or theft, would face expulsion from the clan, which would be signified by crossing out the individual's name from the record. Though the creed was not an official document like a bureaucratic decree, its guidelines served as a loosely binding membership.

My research found that there were several Chew lineages in the Sze Yup region. In Sun-wui County alone, two main clan branches bore the Chew family name. Perhaps, they shared a common ancestor a thousand years ago.

Each branch had its own pedigree. However, the photographic pedigree I acquired belongs to Hoi Mun (海門) branch. There were one hundred fifty pages in all that consisted of two parts: the introduction and genealogical records. The third part was purposely omitted because it is no longer relevant in today's Chinese society.

Four pages of the introduction told the legend of this Chew branch, which traced the family's history back to their original ancestor, Hoi Mun, who is counted as the first generation. He lived in the northern plain of China and was a military general serving in the Song emperor's court in 1100 A.D. After a group of non-Han people called the Jurchen from Northeast China sacked the capital of the Song Empire in 1127, the general and his family fled with the Song emperor to the plain of the Yangzi River Delta where the South Song dynasty was established.

Ever since then, the offspring of the general kept moving southward. Before the Mongol Empire was established in 1271, Hoi Mun's offspring reached the ancient Mei Pass in the northern mountain range in South China, which today is called Kwangtung province.

They first settled in a village called Zyu Gei Hong (珠玑巷) in Nam Hung County (南雄县) on the south side of the foothills of Mei Pass. They lived and worked side by side with seventy other different clans such as the Wongs, Yips, Nanns, Lees, Lows, Yus and many others. It was quite unusual in Chinese society to have so many clans living in one place. Today, thirty-two clans remain living in the ancient village; it has become a legendary shrine for Southern Chinese searching for family roots.

By the end of the thirteenth century, the descendants of Hoi Mun moved southward again to the plains of the Pearl River Delta. Eventually, in the fourteenth century, a smaller branch of this main group settled in a marshland in Sun-wui County. The common and traceable ancestor for this branch was Yun Yeun (源远) a sixth-generation descendant of Hoi Mun, the general.

Legend says that Yun Yeun gave up his aspirations of officialdom for the life of farming and astronomy. He owned a few hundred acres of marshland and turned them into farmland. Later his offspring branched out to the surrounding area in Sun-wui County.

In the mid-sixteenth century, one of Yun Yeun's descendants bought land on the west bank of Tim Gum Creek and began building houses there. Gradually Tim Gum village was formed and became another branch of Yun Yeun's lineage. The village's ancestral temple enshrined Yun Yeun as the original ancestor for Tim Gum lineage.

The story of its generation poem was also detailed in the introduction. The composer was one of Yun Yeun descendants, who belonged to the twelfth generation from Hoi Mun and lived in Tim Gum. His aspiration of officialdom took him down the imperial exam path eight times, but failed. Instead, in 1615 he composed the twenty-character generation poem for Tim Gum lineage that it still follows today. So far, the lineage has reached the last two characters in the poem and I was told a new generation poem was written for future generations.

Up to the twentieth generation, the records in the pedigree were well maintained and detailed. After that, there are blanks or incomplete names. This happened to the Sing generation, the same generation that Wah Lee belonged to. The village name Dong Oin Lei was not even in the record. Perhaps it was too recent to be accounted for.

My heart sank when I could not find the record of our great-grandfather in the clan pedigree. I was unable to locate him according to either his courtesy name or his given name. Only two names from my list of Chinese miners were matched two records in the pedigree. Beside their names, a note was made: "To Gold Mountain in search of fortune." Grandpa Keen's generation was left out.

The omission in the clan records could have been discouraging, but my pursuit of the pedigree was not in vain. I had gained a better understanding of the Chinese naming tradition, which had been lost in history. In the past, the Chinese naming convention followed restricted rules. The given name by parents was reserved exclusively for the person himself and his parents; his courtesy name was for his peers and the general public. It would be inappropriate and disrespectful for younger generations to call our great-grandfather by his given name, Yut Chow, but it is proper for everyone to address him by his courtesy name, Sing Chun. That is the reason why he was not known by his given name in the Cariboo. Instead, his courtesy name is found in the public files and in his grandson's engagement letter. However, his courtesy name was overshadowed by his best-known name, Wah Lee, which became his identity in Canada.

Initially, my dispute of Wah Lee's name was based on a very narrow interpretation of Chinese naming conventions. As I have learned in my research, Chinese naming tradition allows a person to either pick a name voluntarily or be given one by his peers that is associated with a place or business. This name is called an assumed name that can be used in addition to his given name and courtesy name.

For example, a famous Chinese poet, Su Shi, from the Song dynasty, is known by his assumed name Tungpo or "East Hill" because he lived on the eastside of a hill. As for our great-grand-father, Wah Lee may be his assumed name in association with his company. On that note, I concluded my search for the name of Wah Lee. Here is my summary of our great-grandfather's names:

- Given name (名) — 周日潮 Chew Yut Chow, a name chosen by his parents

- Courtesy name (字) — 周升爐 Chew Sing Chun, a name his peers called him

- Assumed name (號) — Wah Lee, a name well known in the Cariboo

The incomplete record of the lineage pedigree put an unexpected end to my search for the history of the Chew clan. Nevertheless, the story of the Keen family had just begun.

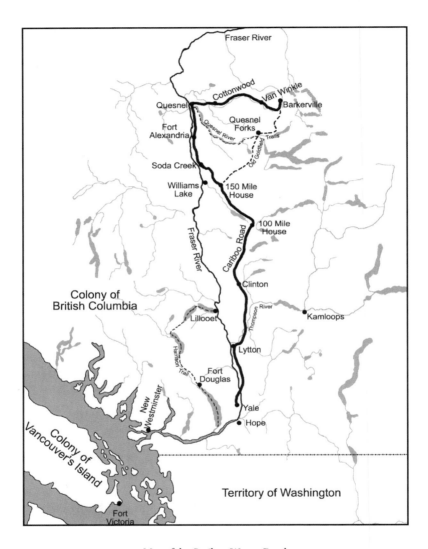

Map of the Cariboo Wagon Road.

FOUR
WAH LEE, THE TRAILBLAZER
(1820–1902)

Very little is known about our great-grandfather's life in China other than these words left by Ah Poh: "He was a *daofu lao* 'tofu maker' (豆腐佬) before he left for Gum San." According to the Canadian census of 1881 and 1891, our great-grandfather was born in 1820 in Tim Gum village in Sun-wui County, China. There is no personal account of him either in China or Canada except for the collective accounts of Wah Lee & Co. that he co-founded with other kinsmen.

His story in this chapter has been pieced together from information drawn from historical books, newspapers and local gazettes. With great respect, I address him in my story as Wah Lee, his better-known name in the Cariboo.

Wah Lee's early life

Born to a traditional Chinese peasant family in a house made of mud, Wah Lee was named Yut Chow, or "tide of the day." As a child, Wah Lee probably obtained his basic education in a village school, which was conveniently located in Tim Gum ancestral temple. The school was partially subsidized by its clan members;

families would still pay a fee to the teacher if they wanted their children to be educated.

Many Chinese believed in education. Even though Wah Lee's father did not have very much, he found a way to finance his son's education in the hope it would give him a better life, or at least make him a respected man in the village. In ancient Chinese society, illiterate peasants looked up to those who had literacy skills. An educated man was held in high regard and expected to uphold and safeguard Confucian codes of conduct, which were often in writing such as the creed in its clan pedigree.

For three or more years, basic education included memorizing and reciting all the verses from a set of Confucian classical books, practicing Chinese writing with a brush pen and learning math tables on an abacus. This kind of learning was not for those who would rather be out in the field than sit in a classroom with a teacher armed with a bamboo strap ready to strike. For a country boy like Wah Lee, the opportunity to go to school was a privilege. He showed his appreciation by doing well.

By the age of twenty, he was referred to as Sing Chun, married his betrothed and started a family of his own. In addition to working his share of the land, he needed to find a way to get ahead and secure his family's future. A common strategy in rural China was to start a cash-earning enterprise such as food processing, weaving or handicrafts. He chose tofu making.

Tofu originated in ancient China thousands of years ago. It is a process in which dried soybeans are turned into soft bean curd by coagulating soymilk. For a long time, it was a home-based enterprise that helped bring in supplementary income to a family. The trick was to sell the product fresh before it spoiled in a warm climate. In the days before refrigeration systems, Wah Lee must have managed the trade very well as he gained a reputation as a *daofu lao*, 'a local tofu maker'.

With his hard work ethic, entrepreneurial skills and determination, Wah Lee would have gained sufficient financial success in due course and could have carried on with his life in the same way as his father or grandfather did before him—tilling and tending the family plot of rice paddies, selling his tofu in the streets of neighbouring villages and towns, and raising a family.

Growing up in the early nineteenth century, Wah Lee would have had no reason to think about going beyond his village or his township, let alone his country. Furthermore, it was un-Confucian for a son to leave home. Historically, travelling outside the country was only for merchants, not peasants like Wah Lee who were bound to the land that was their livelihood.

Coolie trade, peasant revolts and clan war

Beginning in the late eighteenth century, China experienced a big population increase, exploding from 150 million to over 400 million. This was due to a long period of relative peace and the introduction of crops from the New World such as maize, sweet potatoes, tobacco and peanuts. However, the population surge aggravated the chronic shortage of farmland in the Pearl River Delta and gave rise to a surplus of unskilled labourers dubbed "coolies."

On the other side of the globe, demand for cheap labour was high. As the slavery trade was illegal in many western countries by the early 1800s, the colonies began tapping into the cheap labour markets in China. Because of its close proximity to the trading port of Macau, leased to Portugal since 1557, the Sze Yup region turned into a hub to supply coolies to foreign companies from the 1820s onwards.

To escape starvation and poverty, desperate, unemployed Chinese coolies were lured by the promise of employment and wages. Even at the rate of four dollars a month, they signed up as indentured labourers for five to eight years and were shipped out from the port of Macau to Cuba, Peru or Chile to work in the plantations and guano mines. Many of them were never seen again. They had no idea that they were being trapped into debt bondage. This large-scale coolie trade lasted until the 1880s before free immigration took over.

As reported in the *Chinese Recorder and Missionary Journal* in 1888, a coolie cost the shipping company $200, which included contract fee, food, insurance, boat fare and fees charged by a Chinese handler or "crimp." If the coolies survived the long voyage and reached their destination, the shipping company could sell the coolies in a public auction for as much as $350 per head.

Such trade became so profitable that some shipping companies preferred to load coolies rather than crates of silk or tea. During the height of the coolie trade, reports of missing people and abductions were widespread. Sze Yup people used phrases to describe the coolies such as *mia jee zai* 'selling piglets' (卖猪仔) or *jee zai goon* 'piglet pen' (猪仔馆) to describe the horrible stories of coolies who were treated like animals.

Sadly, many of those who were coerced or abducted were trades people. They were locked up in "piglet pens" (barracks) until they were shipped overseas. Families did not know the fate of their loved ones for a long time until a few lucky "piglets" escaped to tell their tales. The Chinese authority did nothing about the abductions and ignored the abusive treatment of coolies. The locals felt very unsafe travelling in their own land.

The coolie trade in the nineteenth century shows how the Qing government was losing its grip on its subjects. The Great Qing Law stated that those who left China would be treated as traitors to the country and face execution on their return home. The large exodus of Chinese coolies signalled the declining power of the Qing government, which at the same time was dealing with an international threat to the country's sovereignty.

Two opium wars with the western powers, the first in 1839–1842 and the second 1856–1860, severely weakened the power of the Qing government. As a result, China lost its major seaports along the coast. The tiny island of Hong Kong at the mouth of the Pearl River Delta was conceded to Britain after the first opium war. In addition to the island, an indemnity of 21 million silver dollars went to Britain.

Besides conflicts with foreign powers, peasant rebellions and civil wars began dominating China's historical landscape for the next hundred years. The largest peasant rebellion in Chinese history took place in 1851. It was called the Taiping Rebellion. Tens of thousands of *chong mo jah* 'long-haired rebels' (長毛賊) from a neighbouring province hoisted a rebellion flag to take on the Qing government and its army.

Letting their hair grow long was an act of rebellion against the Manchu Queue Order, which required a man to shave the crown of his head every ten days and braid the remaining hair into a ponytail. The consequence of disobeying the order was the loss of one's head.

Thousands of longhaired rebels swept northward through seventeen provinces and proclaimed a kingdom of their own, called the Taiping Heavenly Kingdom (太平天国), which controlled the land south of the lower Yangtze valley. The rebellion lasted for fifteen years, from 1851 to 1864, with a death toll of 20 to 30 million people and the destruction of 600 cities and towns.

Although the Sze Yup region narrowly escaped the wrath of the peasants' rebellion, it could not avoid a local revolt in 1854. It was called the Red Turban Revolt because of the red cloth the rebels wore wrapped around their heads. The revolt was led by a highly secretive organization, the Triads, with an anti-Manchurian agenda. Taking advantage of the Taiping Rebellion in the north, the rebels attacked the provincial capital of Canton and sacked its nearby city of Fusan.

Very soon the Red Turban rebels moved into the Sze Yup region. After plundering the county seat of Hoi Ping County, they captured and killed the magistrate, and looted the town before moving on to the next county, Sun-wui. The county seat for Sun-wui was a thousand-year-old town boasting a defense system with walls and a moat. For two months the town was put under siege by tens of thousands of Red Turban rebels. The rebels tried everything, from roadblocks to homemade cannons and explosives, to break through the town but, in the end, the rebels were suppressed by Qing army reinforcements.

What followed was the White Terror carried out by the Qing government. The rebel leaders were hunted down and executed along with their entire families—thousands of rebels were arrested and executed. Those who escaped saved their lives by signing up to be shipped out to South America as coolies.

On the heels of the White Terror, a clan war broke out between two ethnic groups in the Sze Yup region. Known as the Punti-Hakka Clan War, it lasted for twelve years from 1855 to 1866. *Punti* means 'locals' while *hakka* means 'guest family.' Though both groups were Han people and emigrated from the north plains of China, culturally and linguistically they were two different ethnic groups.

Punti people claimed they had come to the area earlier than Hakka people. As a result, they occupied the fertile land while the Hakka people settled in the hillside's less arable land. Over the years, both groups tried to mind their own business. Sometimes territorial conflicts flared up between the two groups, but the local authority usually stamped out the sparks before they escalated into war. These brief skirmishes were not as severe as the twelve-year clan war.

According to the local history, the clan war was sparked during the White Terror by false accusations from both groups that the other clan was supporting the Red Turban rebels. This led to the arrest and killing of people from both groups by Qing government forces. Both groups sought revenge for these deaths on such a scale that the war became an ethnic genocide.

The areas suffering the most were two counties, Toi-san and Hoi Ping, which bordered Hakka territories. Although Tim Gum village did not have any direct impact from the clan war, the surrounding area must have looked like a war zone—human lives lost, bridges and roads destroyed, hundreds of villages burned and fields abandoned. Thousands of male captives from the clan war were sold to foreign companies as coolies while female captives were sent to brothels in Macau. Once again, the coolie trade companies benefitted from human misery.

Wah Lee's dream of making a decent living and securing a future for his family was crushed in the war-torn country by political instability, social upheaval and overall dismal prospects. He began to look somewhere else for his fortune. Luckily, he did not have to look too hard. Far beyond his Tim Gum village and over the South China Sea, a yellow glow rose above the horizon.

Gum San 'Gold Mountain'

Gum San in Sze Yup dialect means "Gold Mountain." There were three *Gum San* where the gold rush took place in the mid-nineteenth century—California, Australia and Canada. Ten years before the Fraser Canyon gold rush in Canada, two main gold discoveries had already sent thousands of men from the Pearl River Delta sailing across the Pacific to foreign, almost mythical lands.

In 1848 news of the discovery of gold in the American River in present-day California travelled fast with a reward that could be understood in any language. Between 1849 and 1850, only a few hundred Chinese gold seekers made their way to California. By 1852 over 20,000 Chinese arrived in San Francisco to seek their fortune.

During the Californian gold rush, new gold fields were discovered on another continent—Australia—and in 1855 tens of thousands of Chinese arrived in Melbourne. The Australian government quickly passed the *Chinese Immigration Act of 1855* to limit the overwhelming numbers of Chinese entering the Victoria gold fields.

To distinguish between the two gold fields, the Chinese nicknamed San Francisco as *Kui Gum San* (Old Gold Mountain) and the Victoria gold fields of Australia, *Sun Gum San* (New Gold Mountain). All these so-called Gum San share one common feature—gold was found in loose sandbars and in the gravel of riverbeds and streambeds. In mining terms, these alluvial deposits were excellent for placer mining, an ancient method of using water to excavate the precious metal.

In Chinese, the term *tou gum* (淘金) vividly depicts placer mining. The Chinese word *tou* (淘) describes the technique of panning, which Chinese peasants were very familiar with, as they used a similar technique to get rid of specks of sand and small rocks in rice by panning the rice in water before cooking. Of course, gold panning was practiced on a much larger scale and required tools such as a spade or shovel, and a gold pan with a flat bottom and slanted sides.

Everyone in Sze Yup was catching the gold fever. Shipbrokers from Macau and Hong Kong found themselves busy setting up ticket agencies in Canton and other major towns in the Pearl River Delta. They began giving out information for the destination as well as selling tickets for the transpacific voyage. The allure of such a journey only increased when a few lucky gold seekers returned home from Gum San showing off their purchasing power, buying land, building new houses, taking more than one wife or holding elaborate wedding banquets for their sons. When the Fraser Canyon gold discovery came along in 1858, the frenzy must have been pushed to a new height.

Most Chinese peasants, including Wah Lee, did not know where California, Australia or the Fraser Canyon was. Nor did they have any experience in gold prospecting, trekking in wildness or living in a harsh Northern American climate. Nevertheless, they were lured by the glowing stories of Gum San and the prosperity it might bring. Even Wah Lee, who was already in his late thirties with a family and perhaps teenaged children, decided to embark on the gold-rush journey. A dozen of his kinsmen from Tim Gum village joined him including Sing Cup (升翁), and probably Sing Joe (升操), Sing Yee (升萱), Sing Chub (升揖), Sing Qin (升逞), Gou Han (高汉), Gou Seen (高美) and Gou Kin (高瓊).

They joined the largest emigration in Chinese history. According to the *Sun-wui Gazette*, the population of Sun-wui County in the year of 1839 was 688,452. By 1907, only 130,000 people lived in the area.

Transpacific voyage

A lyric in a Sze Yup folk song paints a picture of the Sze Yup men who went abroad at that time: "The 'have-nots' went to Havana while the 'haves' ventured to Gum San." (穷人到夏湾, 富人到金山). The have-nots referred to the coolies who were sold like piglets; the haves were those who went abroad on their own accord. In fact, the haves did not have very much at all. What they had was a pair of strong hands, the spirit of determination and diligence.

In the nineteenth century, the transpacific passage fare alone cost at least fifty to fifty-five dollars a person. This price would have been steep for any Chinese peasant, who did not have much to begin with. Some of them borrowed money from labour brokerage companies who would advance the cost of the voyage, called the credit-ticket system. It would take them many years to pay off the debt before they were able to send any money home. Besides the cost of the passage, gold seekers had to reserve some funds for other expenses such as the purchase of provisions and mining tools once they arrived at the destination.

As a peasant and tofu maker, Wah Lee had very little savings. To avoid going to commercial lenders, he would have cashed whatever valuables he had and may have borrowed from his relatives or the clan association. According to the Chew pedigree, their ancestors had reserved ritual land to generate income for the benefits of its members such as paying for education, public works and activities to strengthen its lineage. In the case of a loan to the gold seekers, it would be a good investment for the villagers only if Wah Lee and his kinsmen succeeded. They bore a great deal of responsibility to pay back their clan association and families. Many overseas Chinese repaid their debts by sponsoring relatives or fellow villagers to join them.

For both the borrower and the lender, the uncertainty of return was a gamble that involved great risk. To give a glimpse of how dangerous the voyage Wah Lee and fellow countrymen would have endured, here is a piece of news reported in *The Cariboo Sentinel* on August 27, 1866:

> SAN FRANCISCO, Aug. 14th – *A dispatch was published yesterday announcing the loss of the British ship Fairlight in the China Sea. The Fairlight cleared from this port on Nov. 15th, 1865, for Hong Kong and was on her way back, having sailed from Shanghai on May 29th with a cargo of 600 tons of Chinese merchandise, 227 Chinese*

*and four European passengers. She is supposed to
have gone down with all freight and passengers.*

When it was time to bid farewell to their families, there was not much fanfare. It was rather a sombre occasion, as the families understood once these men were abroad there was no guarantee they would be safe and sound, or that they would ever be seen again. Nor was there a way to know their whereabouts because no postal service existed in the rural countryside in China at that time.

With his family gathered around in the family hall of his mud house, Wah Lee bowed three times in front of his ancestral shrine for their blessings. Afterwards, he joined the others to board the waiting sampan that would sail down the Tam River towards Hong Kong, from where they would sail across the Pacific.

In the mid-1800s transpacific vessels were clipper ships powered by steam with masts and sails to cut quickly through the waves. They were commonly used for cargo shipping. With the influx of emigrants from China, the ships took on passengers in the steerage below deck at a cheaper price than the cabin class. The steerage was typically a cargo space, which was later modified to be an open space, fitted with rows of wooden berths for passengers. The Chinese immigrants shared a similar steerage experience of European immigrants who crossed the Atlantic to the American Continent; only the voyage across the Pacific took much longer.

The transpacific voyage took sixty to sixty-five days from Hong Kong to Port Victoria on Vancouver Island. The fifty-dollar fare bought Wah Lee a space in one of the double berths, excluding bedding, which he provided for himself. He was given a daily provision of two meals of rice and Chinese tea. They cooked the meals in a designated cooking galley in the steerage section. If the ticket agent was kind enough, he would suggest his Chinese passengers bring with them some preserved Chinese vegetables

like *lo bai* (Chinese turnips), salty duck eggs or shrimp paste—
something salty that would help spice up the plain rice. It was a
long voyage at sea without much fresh food on board.

During the two-month voyage, the steerage passengers were
confined below deck for most of the time. Once a day, if the sea
was calm, they were allowed to go onto the upper deck for fresh
air. There was not much to do on board. Many Chinese passengers found themselves spending time lying on their berth,
playing gambling games or having a few puffs of opium or
tobacco in a designated smoking area.

When there was a high wind or gale and the boat rocked, the
steerage passengers endured motion sickness in their berths
or, even worse, the vile smell of someone's stomach evicting its
contents. The daily routine in cramped quarters continued for
weeks on end. There was nothing one could do about the dis-
comforts in the middle of the ocean—the clipper was like a tiny
leaf tossed about in a raging sea.

Once the vessel docked at Port Victoria, Wah Lee and his
countrymen began to prepare for the next leg, a 200-mile
journey to the Fraser River Canyon where the gold fields lay. A
cluster of wooden shacks across from the Johnson Street Ravine
housed Chinese stores, restaurants and clan associations.
Chinese merchants were among the first group of gold seekers
to arrive in Port Victoria. They set up shops and imported
Chinese groceries from San Francisco and Hong Kong. Offering
assistance to the newcomers, they provided temporary lodging
and helped preparation for the journey to the interior. One of
the big Chinese companies was Kwong Lee & Co. known as the
"Chinese Hudson's Bay." Its agents and stores dotted the Cariboo
Wagon Trail.

Wah Lee and his kinsmen would buy most of their supplies
and provisions in Port Victoria, as they must have been warned
that the price of anything on the mainland would be double, or

even triple if they went further north. Chinese merchants were a great help to Chinese miners who were new to the land and spoke not one word of English.

Before long, Wah Lee and other miners set out for the Fraser River gold fields, taking a paddlewheel steamer through the treacherous Georgia Strait from Port Victoria to New Westminster at the mouth of the Fraser River. From there, they continued their trek on foot.

The sight of the Fraser River Valley would have been intimidating to these Sze Yup men who came from a subtropical coastal plain at sea level. The predominant view from the valley was one snow-capped Rocky Mountain peak after another, with the looming shadow of Mount Baker in the background. The mountains were covered by dark forests of sky-reaching firs, dense spruce and jack pine thrusting from rocks and boulders.

Early Chinese miners followed no road but footpaths and trapper trails along the banks of the Fraser River. Wah Lee and his men had to find or make their way through the Fraser River Valley. Though they may have taken pride in the network of rivers and creeks back home, the raging icy water of the Fraser Canyon would have looked much more powerful than the annual flood of the West River in the Pearl River Delta. Bravely, they trudged along the hazardous trail that hugged the river gorge with a straight drop to the torrents below.

Unlike some of the white miners who would have contracted native Indian packers to carry their supplies and provisions, the Chinese miners carried their own, using a bamboo pole across their shoulder just like they would have done back home. Each carried a weight between eighty to one hundred pounds. They usually travelled, worked and lived in groups for the sake of helping and protecting each other.

Chinese miners followed the footsteps of white miners; working abandoned mine claims after the white miners had moved on to another site. In the gold field, it was mutually understood that if a man stopped mining for seventy-two hours, he lost his claim to the site. This unspoken rule enabled Chinese miners to work in the abandoned claims. More often than not, their patience and diligence paid off with reward, perhaps not in the form of nuggets, but in gold flakes or dust.

Wah Lee's first lot in Quesnel

No written account or physical trace of Wah Lee is found in the Fraser Canyon gold fields until the name Wa Lee appears in the *Land Sale Record Book* in 1863. The record shows that Wa Lee purchased a lot in the town site of Quesnel. This is the first solid evidence testifying to his early presence in North Cariboo. It also proves that Wah Lee was in British Columbia at least six to seven years earlier than originally thought. At that time, the Cariboo Wagon Road was under construction but did not reach Quesnel yet.

In 1863 the Cariboo was described in the *British Columbia Guide and Directory* as an extremely rugged and mountainous country that consisted of a large range of mountains, heavily covered in timber. The highest point explored at that time was at least 8,400 feet above sea level and the average elevation was about 5,000 feet. These tall mountain ranges channelled the flow of many rivers and creeks into the Fraser River. The Quesnel River was one of the main tributaries.

This was the fur-trading territory of the Hudson's Bay Company. The main attribute of the Cariboo country was its rich deposits of gold in the creeks and rivers that attracted thousands of men from all corners of the world. The directory reported:

About 1,500 miners were in the Cariboo country during the season of 1861, and the yield of gold has been estimated at $2,000,000. In the early part of the year, 1862, a large emigration from California, Canada and Europe, attracted by the results of the mining season of 1861, flocked to the mines; and it is estimated that 10,000 persons started from Victoria, one-half, however, of whom, deterred by the difficulties of the way, did not succeed in reaching the mining country... This immense crowd coming after an unusually hard winter, during which the transportation was much impeded, almost caused a famine at the mines, and a large quantity of provisions, which in an ordinary year would have reached their destination, was consumed on the road by these unfortunate adventurers.

The Cariboo Gold Rush was actually the second wave in British Columbia. The first wave was the Fraser Canyon Gold Rush that took place mostly in the lower section of the canyon and had a stampede of 30,000 gold seekers from 1858 to 1859. By the year 1860, before the Cariboo Gold Rush began, 25,000 gold seekers had returned home.

A few sites of digging and gold claims in North Cariboo was already reported in 1859, but not enough to be considered another rush until 1861, when gold was struck in Antler Creek and Keithley Creek, north of Horsefly. As reported in the *British Colonist*, large quantities of gold core were discovered north of Quesnelle Forks in June 1861.

The same year, William "Dutch Bill" Dietz found gold in a creek that eventually took his name as Williams Creek. The biggest gold find in the Cariboo was Billy Barker's claim south of Williams Creek in the summer of 1862. A gold mining town began to take shape around the site of Barker's claim; in 1863 the town was named Barkerville.

Many Chinese miners were among the remaining gold seekers after the first gold rush. They kept trekking upstream into the Cariboo region, not far behind the white gold prospectors such as Dietz and Barker. Despite extreme conditions, they were undeterred and made their way to Quesnelle Forks, covering a distance of 400 miles from the mouth of the Fraser River.

When they got to the Forks, their advance north was stopped by white miners who threatened to use violence if they dared venture north of Quesnelle Forks. Many of the Chinese miners stayed south of the Forks; others trekked downstream to the mouth of the Quesnel River.

Meanwhile, the Douglas colonial government was building the Cariboo Wagon Road. By the fall of 1863, the eighteen-foot wide, 300-mile long Cariboo Wagon Road reached Soda Creek from Yale. A sternwheeler on the Upper Fraser River connected the section from Soda Creek to Quesnel. Then, the colonial government had abandoned the original plan to continue the wagon road from Quesnelle Forks to Barkerville; instead, the route picked up from Quesnel via Cottonwood to the new gold town.

Quesnel used to be called Quesnellemouth, not only because of its obvious location at the mouth of the river, but also to distinguish it from Quesnelle Forks ninety miles upstream. Chinese miners used to call it *mou see* (茂士), a direct translation of "mouth." Before the gold rush, this piece of flat land on the junction between the Fraser and Quesnel Rivers was a Hudson's Bay fur trading outpost. By 1863, the outpost was developed into a small settlement with a dozen business buildings, hotels and a sawmill on the east bank of the Fraser River. Kwong Lee & Co. was one of the stores.

With a sternwheeler landing and the extension of the wagon road to Barkerville, Quesnel became a gateway to the gold town. According to the history book *Wagon Road North* written by Art Downs, in early summer of 1863, W. McColl from the Royal Engineers surveyed three town sites around Quesnel, which was marked as Upper, Middle and Lower. Soon after the survey was done, lots were put up for sale in late summer of the same year. The first lot was sold for 400 British pounds.

Wah Lee must have reached Quesnel long before the lot sales. During his journey to North Cariboo, he may have observed how important supplies and provisions were for the miners in the wilderness of B.C.'s interior. Besides the struggle with the harsh weather and battles with sickness and injury, starvation was one of many life-threatening factors facing miners.

As a one-time tofu maker and entrepreneur, Wah Lee saw a business opportunity when the lots were first put up for sale. With twenty British pounds, he bought his first lot—Lot 2 in Block 3. It was located in the north corner between Front Street and Barlow Avenue. Whether he had a vision that Quesnel would become a major transportation centre in North Cariboo or what kind of business he intended to do is lost to history. But one thing is certain that the Keen family history in the Cariboo can trace back as far as August 17, 1863, the day when Wah Lee purchased the lot.

Life in Gold Mountain

Construction of the wagon road from Quesnel to Barkerville commenced in 1864 and was finished in 1865. As a result, more and more Chinese miners moved into the Barkerville area after years of being barred from entering. The town newspaper, *The Cariboo Sentinel*, took notice and published a little note on September 30, 1865: "A large number of Chinese are building houses close to Barkerville, with the intention of becoming residents of Cariboo." The houses mentioned became Barkerville's Chinatown that stretched from the south end of the town.

As Barkerville developed along Williams Creek, the town centre was located on the north side, where most white miners stayed. The gold town in the 1860s was not a temporary mining site but rather a settlement that had everything—churches, hotels, saloons, general stores, dancehalls, restaurants, gambling houses, police station, government assay office and even a courthouse.

In spite of being a latecomer in the new town, Barkerville's Chinatown was quickly taking shape with clan societies, associations, general stores, laundries, restaurants, rooming houses, brothels, opium dens and gambling houses. In 1866 the Gold Commissioner gave a tally of residents in the mining district and came up with the total of 1,261 residents in Barkerville—250 were Chinese—which was recorded by Kwong Lee & Co. This number did not include Chinese miners residing in Quesnel and Quesnelle Forks. In later years, the number of Chinese in the Cariboo region increased to the thousands.

Wah Lee was one of the early Chinese arrivals in Barkerville. On August 1, 1866, he co-founded Wah Lee & Co. and established himself as a merchant conducting business in trade and merchandise in both Quesnel and Barkerville. Wa Lee's Washing & Ironing House captured in Frederick Dally's photograph is the earliest evidence of the company's humble beginning.

A washing house in a gold mining town was a relatively low-cost business. Its operations required a pair of strong hands, water, tubs and scrub boards. The soap was likely made from mixing lard with lye water that could be extracted from a mixture of water and ashes. The cost of an eight-pound press iron would have been the capital to start the business. It was quite ironic that a domestic chore such as laundry usually reserved for women back in China; in Gum San it became a business of men who would make money from. Unfortunately, the washing house was destroyed in the infamous Great Fire of 1868. The business was later rebuilt but in a smaller house.

The washing house was only part of the business operation. The company's ambition was trading and general merchandising, and in 1870 the company obtained licences to sell liquor, retail goods and opium. With the licences, both stores were able to provide rooming house services with opium and gambling dens on site. At that time, opium smoking and gambling were pastimes for many Chinese miners.

Interior of the Wah Lee Store in Barkerville.
(Photo by author)

Wah Lee's one hundred sixteen gold deposit receipts, filed in the government assay office, offered a glimpse of the company's business transactions in the days of gold mining. Solid gold was the main medium of exchange or credit. Many Chinese miners in the Cariboo gold field used the precious metal to trade for their provisions and supplies with Chinese merchants such as Wah Lee & Co., who in turn cashed the gold to pay for the merchandise from the south and delivered them to the Chinese miners.

The business of transportation and disposal of goods in the North Cariboo region was quite a challenge even with the completion of the wagon road. Apart from the length and difficult conditions of the road, the main transportation of goods depended on pack trains pulled by mules or oxen. According to the book *Wagon Road North*, a mule train consisted of sixteen to forty-eight animals. Each mule carried a load of two hundred fifty to four hundred pounds. The average freight rate was forty cents per pound. It took a month for the pack train to travel three hundred seventy-three miles from Yale to Barkerville. A freight outfit was only able to run three trips in a year, from April to October. In other words, stores in North Cariboo had to keep a good stock of supplies and maintain their inventory, especially for the long winter months.

Traditionally, the status of a merchant was placed at the bottom of the social ladder in Chinese society. But in the Cariboo gold fields, Chinese merchants often took on the role of representatives for the Chinese community in the absence of a Chinese consulate, which was not established until 1884. When the newly appointed Colonial Governor visited Barkerville in 1869, Wah Lee & Co. took part in the welcoming committee to represent the Chinese residents. At such an early stage of Chinese life in the Cariboo, the Chinese merchants already realized the importance of being part of the mining community. The committee not only made a welcome speech but also called for a clean up in Chinatown days before the Governor's arrival. The Chinese residents constructed a Chinese style arch in the entranceway of Chinatown to mark the event, a symbol of respect and honour.

Besides being ambassadors for Chinese residents in the gold fields, Chinese merchants often took a leadership role in benevolent associations or societies. Many of them were fraternal organizations following the pattern of clanships or districts back in China. These associations or societies played a very important part in helping their members find employment, providing housing and recreation, and even occasionally settling disputes when issues arose.

Oylin Fangkou (愛蓮房口) in the Cariboo was one such association linked to the Chew clan. According to one Chinese-Canadian history study by Dr. David Chuenyan Lai, the Chew clan was one of the three largest clans during the Cariboo gold rush, especially in the Quesnel area. The other two large clans were the Wongs and the Lis. Oylin Fangkou was also a branch of a larger Chew clan society called Oylin Tong (愛蓮堂) that had been established in China long before Gum San.

The word Oylin 'love of lotus' (愛蓮) comes from a famous piece of prose written by Chew Tun-i (周敦頤), a neo-Confucian philosopher and cosmologist in the Song dynasty who shared the Chew surname. In his prose titled "Love of Lotus Flower" (愛蓮说), Chew Tun-i celebrated the lotus flower as an allegory for moral virtues to be emulated. Although the lotus flower's roots are submerged in mud, when its flower head surfaces above the water, there is no trace of the muddy origins on the petals. Since then, the lotus flower has become a symbol of purity and nobility. Many Chew clans claimed they were related to Chew Tun-i and formed a Chew clanship society called "Love of Lotus Tong" in many parts of China.

Far away from China in the Land of Gold Mountain, branches of Oylin Tong brought the members together to have a place to celebrate festivals, care for the sick and distressed, and find friends in the strange land. Many Chinese miners with the surname Chew, including Wah Lee, were members of the Oylin society. Wah Lee was also entrusted to write letters, send remittances and receive letters from home on behalf of the members.

In the early years in the Cariboo, life was very tough for the Chinese miners who were used to living in a warm climate; only the hope of striking it rich and the support of each other kept them going. Apart from the fear of wild animal encounters, they learned to cope with the harsh winter, which included trudging through four to five feet of snow on snowshoes.

Food shipped from the south was expensive and fresh produce hard to come by. Meat, like chicken or pork, was reserved for special occasions such as Chinese New Year and other Chinese celebrations. To save money, most Chinese kept a monotonous daily diet that included rice, tea, dehydrated or preserved vegetables and some *haam yu* 'salty fish' (咸鱼).

To enhance the flavour in their food and overcome their homesickness, some Chinese found a way to grow Chinese vegetables as well as raise chickens and pigs. Although they were miners, they were peasants before coming to Gum San. By trial and error, patches of green Chinese vegetables soon appeared on the hillside behind the buildings in Barkerville's Chinatown. A couple of Chinese miners went even further; they cleared patches of land on the banks of the Fraser River and tended vegetable gardens. Later they gave up mining and became farmers. The taste of fresh homely food helped ease Chinese miners' homesickness as they adapted to life in North Cariboo.

One of the dishes Chinese residents missed most was fresh seafood, as they grew up in a river delta and fish was part of their diet. When the native people sold fish caught in the Fraser River, the Chinese residents were among the first to purchase them, which also became newsworthy. In May of 1867, *The Cariboo Sentinel* reported:

> *The Indians are selling these fish at the rate of three bucketsful for one bit. The Chinamen, who are always ready with the cash for good cheap grub, are buying it in large quantities, salting, drying and packing them for present and future use.*

The desire to taste familiar food could not be better illustrated than by the monthly pig drive run by Wah Lee & Co. After the completion of the Canadian Pacific Railway in 1885, the trailhead for the Cariboo Wagon Road was relocated from Yale to Ashcroft where the train station was. Dried goods and other merchandise could be shipped at a much cheaper rate; however, fresh pork was impossible to ship. Unwilling to go without pork, the Wah Lee store would run a pig drive from Ashcroft to Barkerville via Quesnel.

The pig drives began after the first snowmelt in the spring and ended before the first snowflakes in the winter. It took a few weeks to cover three hundred miles on foot with a herd of thirty pigs. When the pigs got to Barkerville, they were slaughtered and distributed to the Chinese miners' camps.

Home was always on the mind of Chinese residents in the Cariboo, but a journey back to China proved very expensive before 1872. Besides the costly transpacific passage, a one-way ticket to leave the Cariboo was substantial. Although the stagecoach service started as soon as the wagon road was finished, the fare from Soda Creek to Yale cost one hundred thirty dollars – double the transpacific fare – and the trip took fifty-two hours on a bumpy road. Trekking down on foot was not a good idea because a few dollars in one's pocket might attract unwanted attention.

Many Chinese miners would have stayed in the Cariboo, working and saving until they could make the trip down south and back to China. In 1872 the fare was reduced to sixty-five dollars, half the original price. Perhaps, that was when Wah Lee made his first trip back to China after spending over a decade in the gold fields. There is no written account about his return trip but one proof of his visit was the birth of his son, Chew Keen, in May of 1876.

Wah Lee by then was in his early fifties and a successful Chinese merchant. During his home visit, he purchased farm-land and built new houses in a new village named Dong Oin Lei on the east bank of Tim Gum Creek. He also did the same as many other overseas Chinese did before him—he took a second bride who bore him two sons. Judging from this information, Wah Lee spent a couple of years in China before he returned to the Cariboo.

After his return, Wah Lee remained in the area for another twenty-five years. Some of his kinsmen who came with him in the early years might have pulled up stakes and returned home; others might have left for other parts of British Columbia. In the 1880s, many of the old, large companies left the Cariboo land-scape, including Kwong Lee & Co., which went bankrupt in 1885.

Meanwhile, Wah Lee & Co. was growing steadily in two locations. Wah Lee ran the store in Barkerville and his cousin Sing Cup managed the one in Quesnel. The white residents in Barkerville did not know Wah Lee's given name; they referred to him as "Wah Lee, the big Tyee Chinaman merchant" who would mingle with them whenever there was "a big do or party." The term "big Tyee" means "chief" or "boss" in Chinook Jargon, a pidgin trade language that was widely used in the Pacific Northwest during the nineteenth century.

According to the 1881 census, there were over four hundred Chinese residents living in Quesnel, more than those in Barkerville. The census took place in early April when creeks and rivers were still frozen in the mountains. Many of the Chinese residents including Wah Lee preferred to winter in Quesnel, close to the main road and the provision distribution center. That was the reason why Wah Lee appeared twice in the Quesnel District census.

After many years of "bachelor" life in North Cariboo, Sing Cup married a young Chinese girl in Canada. Her name was Soy Hong. Together, they raised three children in Quesnel—a girl named Ah Haw born in 1887 and two boys, Shong Wing, born in 1889, and Kum Hong, born in 1894.

Wah Lee, who turned seventy-one years old in 1891, never intended to settle in the Cariboo and wished one day to retire in his home village in China if one of his sons could take over his business. And he knew that day would come soon.

Pig drive. (Block print by Jennifer Yip)

FIVE
FROM CHEW TO KEEN (1876–1914)

Over the years, the Keen family assumed the evidence that showed how the family name from Chew to Keen was lost to history until I stumbled upon Grandpa Keen's first immigration record in the General Register of Chinese Immigration database in Library and Archives Canada. My excitement was no less than the moment when I found our great-grandfather Wah Lee's personal names.

"Chu Lai Kin" was Grandpa Keen's name as recorded in the official Canadian document when he first arrived in 1895. Not only were his name, age and certificate number in the file, but his height and physical marks were also detailed. The ignorance of language and culture from both Chinese and English created confusion for future genealogists and historians. Uncle Harry once joked that he got invitations to family reunions from the Irish community because of the family's name, Keen. Perhaps, it was more than a coincidence; there is a running joke that Chinese immigrants were sometimes called "the Irish of the Pacific coast." However, the change from Chew to Keen traces the story of Grandpa Keen's life in both China and Canada.

Call of Gum San

Lai Kin (礼坚) is Grandpa Keen's given name. For some unknown reason, in the immigration office, he provided his given name rather than his courtesy name, Gou Shong (高祥). Later he took Chew Keen (周坚) as his official name in Canada. To his Chinese peers, he was addressed as Gou Shong or Gou Shong Bak (Uncle Gou Shong).

Born on May 17, 1876, Chew Keen grew up in Dong Oin Lei, a new village built with money sent from Gum San. Like many of other children in the Sze Yup region, Chew Keen and his older brother were raised by their mother alone. The regular remittance from overseas reminded them of their father who worked and lived in Gum San, a place far away across the ocean. The brick house his father built provided comfort and security for them and their mother.

The house Wah Lee built was one of the grand houses in Dong Oin Lei with four bedrooms and a formal entranceway. Most of the furniture in the house was made of expensive rosewood. Unlike other houses with entrances from the kitchen porches, Wah Lee's house had a foyer with a formal entranceway that was richly decorated with colourful paintings of birds and flowers, a symbol of status and wealth. The house was the pride of their father, Wah Lee.

With money from overseas, Wah Lee's sons were able to go to school and received a good education. Of the two brothers, Chew Keen must have demonstrated greater learning potential at a young age because he went a bit further than a basic education. He took an apprenticeship with a local Chinese herbalist who taught him how to identify and use Chinese medicinal herbs.

Before the age of eighteen, Chew Keen was hired to teach in the Tim Gum village school where Wah Lee was once a student. One day, he received word from his Gum San father, who asked his son to join him in the Cariboo. Wah Lee, at the age of seventy-four, longed to retire to his home village in China, but not before handing over his business to his son.

The reason he chose his younger son instead of his older son will never be known. Over the years Wah Lee could only monitor his sons' progress from a distance, hoping they were not spoiled by Gum San money. Chew Keen appeared to be a good learner and a respectable young man. He was quick with a Chinese abacus, a necessary skill for a merchant and a great asset for Wah Lee & Co.

After receiving his father's letter, Chew Keen began to prepare for the transpacific trip. One important thing he had to take care of before his journey was to marry his betrothed. It was a custom in the Sze Yup region that a man should get married before he went abroad because he did not know when he would return. Another practical reason for the hastened marriage was that the bride remaining behind would fulfill the traditional Chinese obligations to her parents-in-law in place of her husband.

For the bride, such a marriage was the beginning of many lonely nights, if not years. To Chew Keen, the wedding before his departure was a son's obligation to his family that he would not have questioned. Chew Keen's bride was from a Yu (余) family of some means. Her bound feet were a sign of a proper upbringing and social status at the time.

Soon after the wedding, Chew Keen bid good-bye to his mother, his new bride and the rest of the family, the same way his father did before him. The difference in his journey was that he did not have to raise funds for the trip; his father had taken care of everything, including the fifty-dollar entry fee imposed on Chinese immigrants by the Canadian government after 1885. One of his cousins, Chou Lung, came along with him on the trip. They went to Hong Kong from where they embarked on the *S.S. Tacoma*, a transpacific steamer in December of 1894.

Journey to North Cariboo

This was Chew Keen's first time outside Sun-wui County and his first time on a steamship. He was so amazed by the powerful ocean liner cutting its way through the big swells of waves that he would remember the tonnage and size of the ship in an interview decades later. The journey took only two weeks and the conditions in the steerage compartment had improved considerably compared to the clipper Wah Lee took. At least the steamship was bigger than a clipper.

On January 10, 1895, they arrived in Port Victoria, in the same harbour as his father had done many years before. Their winter arrival meant that the Cariboo Wagon Road was closed and they had to wait until spring. Chew Keen and his cousin spent a few months in Victoria and the Lower Mainland, acclimatizing to the new environment and becoming acquainted with the Chinese community.

By the time Chew Keen landed in Victoria, the old shacks west of the Johnson Street Ravine in Victoria had long gone and replaced with three-storey buildings on both sides of the streets. The area became Canada's first Chinatown, which stretched six city blocks with a population of 3,000 residents. The vibrant business community had over one hundred firms and stores. There were Chinese schools, hospitals, churches and opera houses. Narrow gaps between buildings formed alleyways that led to opium factories, gambling dens and brothels. Chew Keen's short stay on the coast served as a positive introduction to a new country. Chew Keen and his cousin must have felt very much at home within Chinatown. Everywhere they turned, they heard people speaking the same dialect and sharing the same food as the folks back home.

In due time they made their way to Ashcroft where the Cariboo Wagon Road began. Ashcroft had become a major junction for the Cariboo Wagon Road and the Canadian Pacific Railway since 1885. According to Lily Chow's research, at that time there was a fair-sized Chinese settlement in Ashcroft that was not based on gold mining but centred around businesses such as general stores, boarding houses, laundries, restaurants and farming. Also in Ashcroft there was a Chew clan society, which would provide Chew Keen and his cousin with room and board. Once the snow on the road melted, the young men began their long trek to North Cariboo on foot. Wah Lee was waiting for Chew Keen in Van Winkle.

The place named Van Winkle was neither a town nor even a hamlet in the 1890s. In its heyday of early 1860s, Van Winkle served as a main supply station for mining camps in Lightning Creek, with bakers, shoemakers, blacksmiths, hotels, saloons and gambling houses. At one point in time, there was a government post office. Sadly, the community did not last long before it was abandoned. Because of its midway location between Cottonwood and Barkerville on the old wagon road, it remained a stopover for pack trains, where mules and horses could have feed and rest before continuing the journey.

About a mile and a half down Lightning Creek from Van Winkle was Stanley, another mining town. In the 1890s, Stanley was an active gold mining centre with three saloons, four Chinese shops, several gambling houses and an animal corral. In the summer months, the population in Stanley could swell even larger than the one in Barkerville; nearly half the population was Chinese miners.

As usual, Wah Lee & Co. capitalized on the busy season in Stanley by setting up a trading store in Van Winkle close to the activities. It not only helped the company increase trade and merchandise sales, but also allowed it to lay claim to business transactions with various mines and miners.

When Chew Keen and his cousin reached 150 Mile House, they met a partner of the Wah Lee Company, who was herding thirty pigs to Barkerville. He asked the young men to take over the pig drive for the rest of the trip. Years later, Chew Keen would joke that his first job in Canada was pig driving.

Compared to the iconic cattle drive, a pig drive does not sound that spectacular. No legendary cowboys on horseback with lassoes in hand. One could only imagine the two young Chinese men in pointed straw hats, walking behind a drove of thirty pigs, waving their sticks in the air. It took them two weeks to travel one hundred fifty miles to Barkerville. After delivering their livestock, the two men parted. Chou Lung left to pursue gold mining; Chew Keen went to Van Winkle to meet his father. For the first time, father and son would have the opportunity to live together, work together and get to know each other.

Although Chew Keen was a son of Wah Lee, one of the business owners, he received no special treatment; he worked his way up and learned the basic facts of life in this remote corner of the world. One of the tasks was to prepare daily meals for the store staff and boarders. With limited ingredients like plain rice and dehydrated vegetables, he taught himself to make the meals tasty and appetizing. In no time, Chew Keen became a good cook and quite enjoyed the creativity of cooking.

When he was not preparing meals, he learned how to run a general store by observing his father. Chew Keen proved to be as smart as Wah Lee expected him to be. He quickly picked up many aspects of trading and merchandising business in the Wah Lee Company—bookkeeping, ordering and taking inventory. He also managed remittances for Chinese miners. Sometimes he would help the miners who complained about aches or pains with his Chinese herbal medicine.

Placer mining became a thing of the past in the 1890s. Hydraulic mining was the current mining technique, requiring heavy equipment, a team of labourers and investment. Besides the merchandising business, father and son did what was called "grubstake"—investing money for gold prospectors or a mining enterprise in return for a share of the profits. Chew Keen would later recall,

> ... *Over the years he and his father lost more than $250,000 in mines that proved to be little more than moose pasture. One lucky strike north of town proved an exception and yielded up 36 ounces of gold in a day and even at that time gold was worth $16.50 an ounce.*

Chou Lung, Chew Keen's cousin, had more luck; he eventually prospered in gold mining and then returned to China. He later left China again for Gum San in Australia. People went where the gold was.

Chew Keen remained in the Cariboo. For the first couple of years, father and son worked in the Barkerville area, managing the store and trading with miners. One day, word came that Sing Cup was planning to return to China with his family. His older son, Shong Wing, was approaching ten years of age and Sing Cup wanted his son to receive a traditional Chinese education. At that time in North Cariboo, there was no Chinese school. For this very reason, Sing Cup decided to take his whole family back to his village, Kee Gong Li (奇岗里), and left Canada around 1897.

After nearly forty years living in the Cariboo, Wah Lee felt it was time for him to go home. Believing his son would carry on the business he built, he retired to Dong Oin Lei where he enjoyed his golden years surrounded by his family.

Sing Cup died in 1900 at the age of sixty-nine. Wah Lee died in 1902 at the age of eighty-two. Wah Lee left no record of when he arrived or departed from Canada. What he left behind with his son was the legacy of Wah Lee & Co.

Moving to Quesnel

In 1897, after Sing Cup left for China, Chew Keen moved to Quesnel to run the Wah Lee store. Quesnel was then a typical frontier town. Here is how the B.C. Directory described the town in 1893:

> *Quesnel, in the Dominion Electoral district of Yale-Cariboo and Lillooet and Provincial of Cariboo, is beautifully situated at the confluence of the Quesnelle and Fraser Rivers, it is reached by weekly stage from Ashcroft station on the C.P.R., distance 225 miles, fare $37.00. Mail weekly has a telegraph and express office (B.C. Express Co.) Nearest banking point Kamloops. There are four general stores, two hotels, viz; Occidental, Golden Eagle and one church, also a school... Population 150.*

The four stores were Hudson's Bay Co., James Reid General Store, Yan War, and Wah Lee & Co. Many years later, Chew Keen gave a brief description of the stores at that time to a reporter.

Each one (store) sold practically everything from
lumber and groceries to whiskey and beer by the
keg, bottle or glass. All four premises were saloons
where good rye came at two shots for 25 cents. This
was usually taken straight, as water cost 10 cents
a bucket hauled up from the Fraser River. Those
who preferred to carry their cheer home could get
it for 75 cents a bottle and Hudson's Bay Co. rum
was $4 a gallon. This was the over proof variety.

Soon after Chew Keen settled in Quesnel, he did something different from his father—he hired a local schoolteacher, Mrs. Earley, to teach him English. Mrs. Alice Earley was the first appointed teacher in the Quesnel public school. The town of Quesnel itself was very small in the 1890s. The population of one hundred fifty residents was made up of people from different nationalities such as French, Irish, Swedish, Scottish, German, American and a few dozen Chinese. They communicated with each other in English; even the Chinese residents would pick up a phrase or two.

Chew Keen must have realized the language skill would be a great benefit to Wah Lee & Co. and better bridge the communication gap between the two communities, Chinese and English. Unlike many Chinese residents who learned their broken English through daily contact, he wanted to learn the language properly. Chew Keen took private English lesson from Mrs. Earley for a few years.

In 1899 Chew Keen applied for naturalization. As stated in the British naturalization and citizenship law, aliens who lived for five years in Britain or its colonies such as Canada could apply for naturalization and become British subjects. Many of the successful Chinese merchants and long-time Chinese residents with good standing in Canada applied and were usually granted citizenship. No physical record of Chew Keen's naturalization can be found but he was listed in the 1901 national census as a naturalized British subject.

One very important piece missing in the naturalization process was the franchise—the right to vote. From 1872, Chinese residents in British Columbia were banned from voting. When Chew Keen applied for naturalization, he did not think too much about what that missing piece implied because he regarded himself as a sojourner who would eventually return to his home country.

In the spring of 1901, the name "Chew Keen" was registered for the first time in the national census. After that, "Keen" became the family name. The census revealed that, at the age of twenty-six, Chew Keen was the manager of the Wah Lee store in Quesnel with annual earnings of three hundred sixty dollars. He worked seventy hours a week and lived above the store with nine other Chinese residents, including two store clerks, a cook and six Chinese lodgers who worked as farmhands, miners or labourers.

At the turn of the twentieth century, gold mining gradually gave way to farming. Many miners, Chinese included, quit mining and began to farm. Many of the remaining Chinese in the Cariboo region were labourers hired to do work such as digging ditches, splitting wood or other jobs related to mining. According to Bill Hong, a long-time Chinese resident in Barkerville, Wah Lee & Co. was one of the five Chinese stores in the Cariboo region supplying Chinese labourers to the mining companies for their various projects.

In 1907, one of Sing Cup's sons returned to Quesnel after spending some years in China. Quesnel residents called him C.S. Wing, short for Chew Shong Wing. During his time in China, he received a Chinese education, got married and acquired photography skills. In the early twentieth century, cameras were new gadgets from Gum San and professional photography studios were popular in the Sze Yup region.

Upon his return, eighteen-year-old C.S. Wing turned one of the rooms in Wah Lee store into a photography studio. He took many portraits of the local people and developed the prints in his studio. With a combination of practical business and artistic flare, he also photographed scenery in the Cariboo region, printed it on postcards and sold them in stores.

With C.S. Wing's return, Chew Keen decided to take a much-deserved trip back to China. His first wife, Yu Shee, had been waiting for his return for nearly fifteen years. In Chew Keen's absence, she had fulfilled her duty as a daughter-in-law, looking after Chew Keen's parents and family. But one concern for Yu Shee, as well as Chew Keen, was having children. After all, Chew Keen had departed for Canada in such a hurry after their wedding; they had no time to start a family.

In old China, marriage was a pragmatic affair, conducted for the purpose of procreation—in particular, the birth of a son. In Confucian belief, producing male heirs was the most important measure of a good son. Chew Keen, as a filial son, would have felt the pressure to have a son to fulfill his family duties and obligations.

Like his father before him, there is no account of Chew Keen's first return visit to China. Only his oldest son's birth in 1910 provides evidence of his presence in Dong Oin Lei between 1908 and 1909. With his mother's approval, Chew Keen took a second bride from a Yip family during his first home visit.

Polygamy was a common practice in old China and perceived as necessary for family survival, growth and prestige, if one could afford it. As a result, many elite overseas Chinese merchants had more than one wife. One example was Yip San, a well-known merchant in Vancouver and also my father-in-law's grandfather. He took four wives and brought three of them back to Vancouver. Chew Keen's wives did not disappoint him or his family; both had become pregnant during his visit. However, Chew Keen did not wait to see his newborns. A new business opportunity for his company awaited him in the Cariboo.

Before his trip to China, the partners of Wah Lee & Co. must have discussed new plans for the company's development. Part of their ambition was to restructure and expand the company's operation to Hong Kong and the Sze Yup region. While Chew Keen was visiting his family, he was probably gauging how favourable business conditions were in China to support the expansion of the company.

Wah Lee General Store

In 1909 the population of Quesnel jumped from one hundred fifty to five hundred. The town also had its own weekly newspaper, the *Cariboo Observer*, which was first published in August of 1908. It was never hard-pressed to find stories to write about; the lives of the town residents provided plenty of news from personal whereabouts to international events. Wah Lee & Co. was a regular patron of the newspaper, advertising its merchandise in nearly every issue.

Soon after Chew Keen returned from China, the old partnership of the company was dissolved. In 1910 a new partnership was created with thirteen individuals, each owning one share. In the new agreement, five individuals had holdings in the Barkerville store. Chew Keen, C.S. Wing, Dear Sut Sing and Chew You Len had holdings in the Quesnel store. The company also had four new investors from Hong Kong, who named Chew Keen as their attorney. The new partnership was formally notarized on October 10, 1911. The holdings of the Wah Lee store in Barkerville were sold to Sing Kee Company in 1913. Regrettably, the store was destroyed in a fire in 1914.

Wah Lee & Co. in Quesnel remained in the hands of Chew Keen, C.S. Wing and other partners. At the age of thirty-six, Chew Keen was the owner/manager. He still worked seventy hours a week, fifty-two weeks a year, but now his annual income increased to seven hundred sixty dollars. According to the census in 1911, he was the head of the household and lived with fifteen other people. Actually, the "household" was the Wah Lee store and it included his business partners: thirty-two-year-old Chew You Len, who was listed as a storekeeper; sixty-three-year-old Dear Sut Sing, also a storekeeper; and twenty-two-year-old C.S. Wing, a cook.

The general population in Quesnel had increased gradually while the Chinese population dwindled to a small number of fifty. They worked as cooks, laundrymen, water carriers and farmhands. With the shrinking number of Chinese residents in Quesnel, Wah Lee & Co. focused on integrating into the local town life and serving the general public. The company often sponsored local events like the annual Farm Fair and made donations to the construction of the new hospital and athletic clubs.

At the beginning of 1914, Wah Lee & Co. decided to expand its operation and build a new two-storey general store with a basement. Its location was on the corner of Reid Street and Barlow Avenue, close to Quesnel's business quarter. The local construction company Joyce & Anderson commenced the work. In May 1914, the new sixty-by-seventy-foot Wah Lee & Co. building was completed and furnished with a telephone service. The address was P.O. Box 25 and the telephone number was 4a.

Wah Lee Store building on the corner of Reid Street and Barlow Avenue, ca. 1915.
Photo by C.S. Wing (Author's collection)

The new store design was unusual, as the family would later recall.

> *It was the largest general store in Quesnel, which was made of log construction and faced west with the back on Reid Street. The ceiling reached fifteen feet high with a mezzanine floor where Chinese boarders slept, especially in wintertime when they made their homes along the side that ran along the north wall under the eaves of the roof. Also on the mezzanine floor, there was a cabinet with many small drawers full of Chinese herbs standing against one wall. The entrance door was locked at night with a wooden bar set in two iron clevises. The counter started just inside the door to the right and ran along the south wall. The string for tying parcels was suspended in a basket from the ceiling with the end hanging down within reach*

of the clerk. Sometimes the high ceiling would be used to suspend the raw bananas until they were ripened. Just inside the door by the counter, there was a high stool. As it was near the lamp used by Chew Keen to do his accounts, his guests would sometimes sit there to read Chinese newspapers. A cook was hired to make meals for the staff and the lodgers.

The company also issued its aluminum trade tokens with the Wah Lee store name on them in different denominations from five cents to ten dollars. The idea of trade tokens was not new to Wah Lee & Co. The Hudson's Bay Company had been issuing its own trade tokens since 1840. Merchants in small towns in North America used them to promote trade and credit to customers. With the low cost of aluminum production after 1890, the Wah Lee store might have adopted the idea for the convenience of their customers. It was a very smart business idea to tie the token holders to the store.

The Wah Lee Store trading tokens circulated in North Cariboo at the turn of the twentieth century. Chew Keen donated the last 12 remaining store tokens to the Quesnel Museum in 1957. (Courtesy of the Quesnel Museum)

The new Wah Lee store kept pace with development in B.C.'s northern interior in the early twentieth century. Sixty miles north of Quesnel, the Grand Trunk Pacific Railway was under construction in Fort George (today's Prince George), which generated some excitement in the small town. Wah Lee & Co. even bought a piece of property in South Fort George in 1913 when lot sales were advertised in the newspapers.

Quesnel residents could hardly wait for the arrival of the Pacific Great Eastern Railway, which was supposed to connect with the Grand Trunk Pacific Railway in Fort George. The construction had already started in 1912 from North Vancouver, which brought great hope to the town of Quesnel. On October 10, 1914, a piece of realty news appeared in the local newspaper:

> *A.E. Boyd has moved from the Thompson cottage*
> *to the new one next door recently erected by R.C.*
> *Mitchell. Mr. Mitchell recently sold this property to*
> *Mr. King, of the Wah Lee Co.*

Apparently, Chew Keen bought a piece of residential property, which was possibly the house on the 500 block of Reid Street in Quesnel North. He had been sharing living space with store staff and lodgers in the Wah Lee store since he came to Canada. The purchase of a residential house indicated he had a plan for its use in the future.

In July of 1914, a global war broke out in Europe. Canada, as part of the British Empire, entered the war in August 1914. Everything came to a halt as young men went off to war. The construction of railways stopped and every effort was put into supporting the war.

A year later, on July 24, 1915, Chew Keen took leave from the company as the *Cariboo Observer* announced in the "persons whereabouts" column:

> *Chew Keen, local manager for the Wah Lee Co., Limited, left yesterday for Hong Kong, China, where he expects to spend the next six months.*

Chew Keen's C.I.9 Certificate, 1915. (Database of Immigrants from China, 1885-1949, Library and Archives Canada, e008274063)

SIX
GUM SAN VISITOR (1915–1917)

Chew Keen's family in China did not have to wait for another fifteen years before his next home visit; it was only another five years until he came back. However, within those five short years, the world had changed immensely, especially in China. In 1912, a young Republic of China was born. After ruling for two hundred sixty-eight years, the Empire of the Great Qing was abolished ending two thousand years of Imperial China. From afar, the overseas Chinese welcomed the changes in China and were happy to cut off the long queue that symbolized their subjugation to the Qing rulers.

As China tried to forge its political path, the rest of the world plunged into the First World War, known as the Great War. When Chew Keen embarked on his home journey, the war had been raging in Europe for a full year. Fortunately on the Pacific side, everything was relatively calm and the transpacific passage was uninterrupted.

Home visit

Before boarding his ship for Hong Kong, Chew Keen had to take care of a few things in Vancouver such as his travel document and gift shopping for his family. Immigration rules in Canada were tightening up. Over the years, the government had issued a number of different certificates to Chinese immigrants. Now, a person of Chinese ancestry who wished to leave Canada temporarily was required to register with immigration authorities and get a Certificate of Leave called C.I.9. To comply with the new rule, Chew Keen had to surrender his current C.I.36 Certificate for a C.I.9 Certificate. Upon his re-entrance to Canada later, he would hand in his C.I.9 for the return of his original certificate.

When Chew Keen first arrived in 1895, he paid a fifty-dollar entrance fee. Since then, the entrance fee for a new Chinese immigrant had increased to five hundred dollars, a measure to discourage new Chinese immigrants coming to Canada. The Chinese called the fee a head tax; it was imposed only on Chinese immigrants. On the C.I.9 certificate, Chew Keen signed his Chinese name in the English name order "Keen Chew" instead of "Chew Keen".

"Never return home with empty hands," the overseas Chinese often said. Not only was it a matter of being rude and ungrateful towards your family, but also a home visit without gifts was an admission of failure that would bring shame to the family. Those who could afford a return trip home were expected to bring gifts—trunks of them.

Because of this, some shops in Chinatown offered customers a convenient gift-packing service. With a simple request from its customer, the shopkeeper would collect all the most popular items of the time and pack them into sturdy trunks that could withstand the long and rough ocean voyage.

The gifts they packed tended to be practical and functional everyday items such as clothing, shoes, bath soaps, kettles, aluminum pots, knives, washbasins and candles—things the family needed and something to please everyone. In China, they were considered luxury items and were most welcome gifts. If any room were left in the trunk, treats such as oranges and candies would be thrown in.

A home visit cost not only a steamer ticket, but also hundreds of dollars for gift giving. The financial burden of such a trip deterred many overseas Chinese from visiting their homes until they could save enough to cover such expenses. Even Chew Keen, a merchant, did not make regular trips to his home village.

The long absences from home changed the overseas' status in the village. When they came home, they were referred to as *hakk* 'visitors' (客). To tell where they came back from, the locals had different labels for them. *Nanyang hakk,* 'South China Seas guest' (南洋客) was from Java, Malaya or Boneo. *Hong San hakk* 'sandalwood mountain guest' (香山客) was from the Hawaiian Islands. *Gum San hakk* 'gold mountain guest' (金山客) was from the United States, Canada or Australia. Chew Keen was a *Gum San hakk.*

With trunks of gifts secured, Chew Keen finally boarded the *S.S. Monteagle* on August 8, 1915, sailing for Hong Kong. The whole voyage from Canada to China took less than three weeks. After disembarking at Hong Kong harbour, he would take a boat to his village. He arrived in Dong Oin Lei by the end of August 1915.

Great changes had taken place in his home county since his last visit. Apart from the new Republic of China, Sun-wui County, or the Sze Yup region for that matter, had asserted itself as a place of development and progress. The main section of Sunning Railway from Toi-san to Sun-wui had been completed and in service. In Da Zap market town, two-storey and three-storey buildings had replaced the old palm and bamboo huts and were modeled after the European style. The price of grain was stable and affordable. Cantonese opera was popular in market bazaars, and more children were able to go to school.

Sze Yup's prosperity resulted from the money pouring in from abroad. The locals called it *Gum San E'ng* (金山银) or 'gold mountain money,' a phrase that evoked images of streets paved with gold. The term *gum san* became a prefix for everything that came from overseas—gum san candies, gum san oranges, gum san candles and gum san pots. Even the trunks and the rope that held them together were called gum san trunks and gum san rope.

In Dong Oin Lei, Chew Keen's family was anticipating his homecoming. His mother, Sing Chun Mou, was alive, well and still in charge. She would have picked an auspicious date for the ancestral homage and ordered a roast pig for the special occasion. Words of invitation were sent out to relatives and friends for a welcoming feast. Everyone was jubilant about welcoming Chew Keen home.

Chew Keen's two wives, Yu Shee and Yip Shee, were more excited than anyone. Receiving a second visit from their husband after such a short time made them feel very happy and lucky. Many wives of overseas Chinese did not get to see their husbands as often as they wished. They called themselves "widows" of living husbands absent from home.

During Chew Keen's last visit, both Yu Shee and Yip Shee became pregnant. When his children were born, he had already returned to Gum San. Now the mothers could present their children to their father for the first time. Both children were five years old, perhaps only a few months apart. His son from his first wife was named Lung Gong (龙光). The daughter from his second wife was called Kin Bao (琼宝).

They all lived in the house that Wah Lee built. There were more than enough rooms for the family of three generations. Sing Chun Mou, Chew Keen's mother, occupied one bedroom; his first wife, Yu Shee, shared one bedroom with her son; his second wife, Yip Shee, in another with her daughter. And there was still a spare room. Each bedroom was furnished with an elaborately decorated six-post bed that had painted panels with red-and-gold trim. Each room had a loft that stored the family most valuable commodity – rice. Rice was the most popular grain in Southern China, which was not only stable food, but also used for trade in the market. Under the supervision of Sing Chun Mou, the women lived under the same roof, shared household chores, raise children and had their meals together.

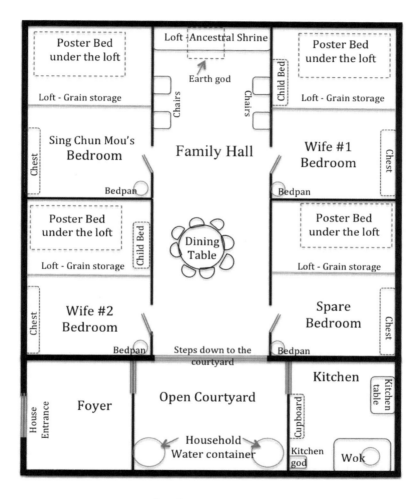

Wah Lee's house interior layout.

The homecoming feast must have been a big celebration with relatives and friends from nearby villages and towns. Family and invited guests would look forward to seeing what gifts were brought from Gum San. Chew Keen's story of this special occasion is lost, but other families with overseas Chinese remember theirs.

Family members and friends, even onlookers, would gather around in the family hall waiting for the trunks to be opened. One by one, each gift would be pulled out as if it was a surprise from a magician's hat. One coveted item was the candle. Back then, there was no electricity and oil lamps were expensive. Gum San candles were special; they lasted longer than the local ones. Everyone walked away very happy with whatever came from Gum San. Even the little kids were pleased with a couple of Gum San candies. In return, the invited guests would bring a life chicken, duck or goose as a thank-you gift.

As reported in the *Cariboo Observer*, Chew Keen originally planned to be away for six months. Instead, his home visit lasted over a year. There was a lot of happening during this trip, both personal matters and family issues.

Chew Keen must have been contemplating the idea of returning to Quesnel with a wife. Like his father before him, he had lived a bachelor's life in the Cariboo, even though he was a married man with two wives and children. During the gold mining era, very few Chinese families lived in North Cariboo because of the harsh living conditions and its remoteness. That was in the past. Since Chew Keen arrived, life in the Cariboo had improved, especially with the arrival of automobiles and electricity.

In Quesnel, there was a town hospital staffed with a highly respected doctor, Dr. Baker, and his team of nurses. Business in Wah Lee & Co. flourished and the general merchandise store was the largest in the area. What gave Chew Keen hope for a family life was the construction of the two railways – one from the north and the other from the south. These railways would connect Quesnel to the rest of the world, making it more accessible and help local business and trade. Compared to Victoria or Vancouver, he was fully aware that Quesnel was still a frontier town, but he would not discount it as a place to raise a family. The question was, who in the family would be willing to return with Chew Keen to live in the Cariboo?

Neither of Chew Keen's wives were ideal candidates. His first wife had bound feet and his second wife was pregnant with her second child. Besides, his young children were at the school age and in need of their mother's care. The yearning for a family life was so strong that Chew Keen decided to take a third bride. He hoped she would be young and strong, a woman who was physically fit to live in North Cariboo.

Finding a willing bride was not hard at that time in the Sze Yup region. More often than not, a family wanted to marry their daughter to a Gum San man rather than someone of the girl's own choice. As a local folk song attests,

> *Never let your daughter marry a peasant*
> *Whose head is full of dirt and feet with cow patty;*
> *Quick, marry her to the Gold Mountain man*
> *Who will return with tons of money.*

In some extreme cases, the family so desperately wanted their daughter to marry a Gum San man, they did so even in the groom's absence. At the wedding, they would use a rooster in place of the Gum San groom. Some wives never met their husbands for their entire married life. The only proof of her husband's existence would be the remittance he sent home.

After Chew Keen expressed his intention of finding another wife, a resourceful matchmaker was consulted. Matchmaking was a profession mostly reserved for women who not only had keen eyes and ears, but also possessed the special qualities of being quick-witted and a go-getter with thick skin. It was not a job for a reserved, shy person.

With a simple request for Chew Keen's courtesy name, birthday and Chinese zodiac sign, the matchmaker would gladly help him find a bride in no time. The zodiac sign of a person, male and female, was an important part in a blind marriage. The matchmaker would check the couple's compatibility with the Eight Trigrams. Once a match was found, the matchmaker would notify Chew Keen and play the role of a go-between. Chew Keen's match was a girl from the village of Baw Hop in the Kongmoon District.

Low Mon Ho 刘晚好

Low Mon Ho (刘晚好) was the maiden name for Chew Keen's third wife. Low was her family name and Mon Ho was her given name, meaning 'good evening' in English. Born on November 4, 1899, Mon Ho was girl No. 5 in her family. No one in the Keen family knows anything about her father. He may have been one of thousands of other Sze Yup men who worked overseas and supported his family by remittances.

As the youngest girl, Mon Ho grew up in a relatively carefree home with her mother, sisters and a younger brother. She was lucky that foot binding had been outlawed in China by the time she came into the world. Like millions of other girls and women in China at that time, she never went to school to learn to read and write. But she learned local folk songs and rhymes by heart from her mother, older sisters and girlfriends in the village. Her talent was sewing by hand. She helped her family earn extra income by making and mending clothes for the locals.

According to the custom in the Pearl River Delta, when a girl entered puberty she would move into a girls' room called *mui zah aoh* (妹仔屋), where sisters and female cousins gathered and shared the sleeping space in a dormitory style until they were married. During the day, the girls spent time in their own homes. When night fell, they retired to the girls' room where they would catch up on daily gossip and stories.

This room became a so-called night school for young girls like Mon Ho learning about the world beyond the walls of their homes and village. Sometimes, married women who came to visit their families could stay overnight in the girls' room. A night with a married woman could be an eye-opening experience for the young girls, who would listen wide-eyed to the woman's life stories, good and bad—stories of marriages gone wrong, irresponsible husbands gambling away family wealth, or horrible birthing experiences. Most of the time, the girls shared dreams of a life of luxury as a *Gum San poh*, a nickname for a wife of an overseas Chinese. Two of Mon Ho's older sisters had married Gum San men; Mon Ho felt that one day she would follow their footsteps. That day came sooner than she expected.

In those days, girls and boys in the Sze Yup region used to get married at a very young age, about fifteen or sixteen years old. Arranged marriages were the norm. Some were arranged in infancy, others in early teens. Following the *Book of Rites*, a proper and respectable marriage should follow a six-step etiquette:

- Step 1—formal proposal
- Step 2—requirement of the bride's name and birth date
- Step 3—compatibility with eight trigrams
- Step 4—betrothal gifts to the bride family
- Step 5—selection of an auspicious wedding date
- Step 6—wedding ceremony

Every step was governed by strict rules and traditions. One step out of line, it was believed, would bring bad luck. With these complexities, it was no wonder a matchmaker was hired for the marriage business.

With so many girls in the family, matchmakers must have frequented their house and made routine request. But Mon Ho's mother was not in a hurry to marry her youngest daughter. She waited until Mon Ho reached the age of sixteen before putting the word out to the matchmakers. All was supposed to be arranged without consulting the bride-to-be. Mon Ho, by accident, stole a glimpse of her future husband before the wedding. She later told her daughter, Beatrice, what had happened.

It was the day when Chew Keen came to visit Mon Ho's mother. He brought betrothal gifts to his future bride's family and confirmed the wedding date at the same time. Mon Ho happened to be in the family hall with her mother and one of her married sisters when Chew Keen arrived with the matchmaker. Traditional Chinese propriety required any maiden to withdraw from a situation where a strange man was present. Quickly, Mon Ho and her sister slipped into their mother's bedroom adjoining the family hall and hid inside while their mother greeted the guests.

The bedroom door was open except for a curtain hanging on the doorframe, serving as a privacy screen. Both sisters could hear the conversation between their mother and the matchmaker. Being curious, Mon Ho could not help taking a peek in the hall through the small gap between the curtain and the doorway.

She saw a man in a western style suit over a white shirt, sitting quietly by the tea table. He did not say much except for some polite greetings. Mon Ho could not get a good look at him, but his glasses and mild, quiet manner told her he was an educated gentleman. Before Mon Ho could learn more about him, the guests rose to take their leave.

Local traditions and custom in Southern China dictated what betrothal gifts should include. Many items were ordinary groceries such as chickens, pork, fish, nuts, rice wine, tea, sesame seeds and fruits. The expensive and special items were a showcase of various dried goods and dried seafood, such as hair moss, shiitake mushrooms, abalone, oysters, scallops, shrimps, squids, sea cucumbers, shark fin and fish maw. And of course, the future groom would leave a bride price in a big red envelope for the future mother-in-law. For the bride's relatives, dozens and dozens of sweetmeats would also be handed out. As the Chinese saying goes, "A wedding can wipe out a man's life savings."

Shortly after Chew Keen's visit, Mon Ho was told the man was her future husband, a merchant from Gum San. His family lived in Dong Oin Lei village in Da Zap Township. Mon Ho also learned that her future husband intended to take her with him to Gum San, which might have helped her accept the news that she was to be Chew Keen's third wife.

For a girl of barely seventeen, marriage would be a life-changing event. Mon Ho had very little time to get prepared; everything happened so fast from that fateful date. In three months, she would be out of the girls' room and become a Gum San poh.

Following Sze Yup traditions, a few days before the wedding, Mon Ho would have spent her last maiden days together with her sisters, cousins and girlfriends in the girls' room, singing bridal songs—songs of lament rather than happy tunes. There would be no set lyrics to follow; they simply made up the words or lines as they sang along to the melody.

The lyrics expressed the bride's gratitude to her parents, her sad good-bye to her sisters and brothers, her good times with her girlfriends and her wishes about her unknown future home. If the girl did not like the marriage arrangement, she would curse the matchmaker in her song. As they sang, they would cry; thus, the local women called it "The Bridal Lament." For many Chinese girls, marriage was the end of their carefree life and the beginning of a life that belonged to someone else.

On her wedding day, Mon Ho rose at dawn for her headdress ceremony, an ancient Chinese ritual of womanhood. First, a woman came to pluck all Mon Ho's facial hair with a fine string before applying make-up. Next, a "good-luck woman" combed Mon Ho's long hair with special oil and coiled it in a bun at the back of her head—a symbol of a married woman. This good-luck woman usually had a good standing in the community and exemplified good fortune, not necessarily measured by wealth, but by her happy family, a family with three or four generations living under the same roof. She would use a brand new comb to perform the hairdressing ritual, singing "The Hair Combing Song" with all the best wishes to the bride in her married life.

Finally Mon Ho entered the family hall in her bright red Chinese wedding dress with elaborate embroidery, called a *cheongsam*. She bowed three times—once to Heaven and Earth, once to her ancestors and once to her mother. For the last time as a maiden, Mon Ho knelt down to serve her mother a cup of tea before she was escorted to the waiting wedding sedan. With a red veil draped over her head, she was carried away to her husband's village, Dong Oin Lei, twenty kilometers away from her home village.

An eventful year

During Chew Keen's home visit, a few events took place in addition to his marriage to Mon Ho. In the summer of 1916, his second wife, Yip Shee, gave birth to Chew Keen's second son, Lung Shong (龙骧). As the family was expanding, Chew Keen's responsibility was growing. Not only did he have to take care of his own family, his older brother's family was also in his care. According to the family source, after Chew Keen's brother died, his sister-in-law had remarried leaving her two children in Dong Oin Lei. Without any hesitation, Chew Keen took them in.

Now he was the head of a household of ten—his mother, three wives, three young children, a niece and a nephew. All the responsibilities and obligations were laid on Chew Keen's shoulders. Gum San money secured the financial part. But family safety was a main concern not in Chew Keen's control. His worry was deepened by the political instability of China.

Shortly after his arrival in China, Chew Keen witnessed the rise and fall of the short-lived, self-proclaimed Empire of China (1915–1916). A powerful military general attempted to reinstate monarchy in China, but the emperor's sudden death only gave him a reign of eighty-three days. It also marked the beginning of the warlord era, in which China was divided and controlled by military cliques. Battles for a unified Republic of China were on and lasted for the next decade. As a result, Chinese people suffered the ill effects of government infighting and a lawless society for a long time.

Reports from incidents of being mugged in the woods to village raids at night became frequent in Sze Yup region that Chew Keen began to worry about his family's safety. Potentially, villages such as Dong Oin Lei could become bandits' easy target because many men went abroad and left their women and children at home. The village was not built like a fort with walls, moat and escape routes. The open plan of the village meant that it could be accessed from almost everywhere. Chew Keen had to make an emergency plan for his family before leaving for Canada. Meanwhile, he was attending to another urgent matter.

A violent incident took place within Tim Gum's Chew clan during Chew Keen's visit. Tim Gum was the ancestral village that gave rise to other villages, such as Dong Oin Lei and Key Gong Li. The villagers in Tim Gum had been living together for centuries, and family feuds and disagreements were impossible to avoid. In the past, the elders would settle a conflict or dispute before it escalated. According to the pedigree, only once in the village's history did a dispute between two brothers result in a loss of life.

This time, a verbal argument over some territorial issues between two parties led to a physical altercation resulting in the death of a kinsman. It ripped open an old wound inflicted centuries ago among the clan members. The deceased belonged to a family that was related to Chew Keen's family branch. They called for a new village, away from the bullying family. To build a new village was a group effort and needed financial support from everyone, especially those abroad.

A planning committee was established for fundraising, site selection, land and material purchase, and construction. Amongst his peers, Chew Keen was considered an educated man and a successful merchant in Gum San. Since he was in town, he was involved in the site selection committee. With the help of a Feng Shui master, the committee scouted locations for the new village.

Letters were sent out to related family members in places such as Philip Bay in Australia, as well as Quesnel and Toronto in Canada, asking for their financial commitment by pledging how many houses they wanted. Chew Keen had pledged for four houses for his own family and one house for his nephew. Each house cost ¥3,000. In those days, the communication back and forth between China and overseas took a while. Before anything was resolved, Chew Keen found himself spending his second Chinese New Year in Dong Oin Lei.

After the Chinese New Year celebration in 1917, Chew Keen learned his first wife, Yu Shee, was pregnant with her second child. But he could not stay any longer in China for he needed to go back to Canada and make money to fulfill his family obligations and pledge for the houses.

In mid-March of 1917, Chew Keen and Mon Ho said goodbye to the family and took the train to Kongmoon and, from there, a boat to Hong Kong. Mon Ho brought with her two family photographs—a portrait of her mother and a photo of her two married sisters with her nephew and niece.

Mon Ho's mother, ca. 1917.
(Courtesy of the family)

Mon Ho's two sisters with her niece and nephew, ca. 1917.
(Courtesy of the family)

Quesnel in 1920. A view from the west bank of the Fraser River.
(Courtesy of the Quesnel Museum)

SEVEN
FAR AND AWAY FROM HOME

Mon Ho's going to Gum San with her husband would have been the envy of many Gum San poh who remained behind to look after their in-laws and families. But the thought of travelling to an unknown place, leaving her family and everything familiar behind would have terrified Mon Ho, who had never travelled beyond her home county before. The concept of the distance between China and Canada was beyond her grasp. From the day she married Chew Keen, her fate was sealed with his. Now, on this unknown journey, she could only put all her faith in her husband.

Mon Ho's journey to Gum San

It was a short trip from Sun-wui to Hong Kong where they expected to board a ship to Canada right away. After their arrival in Hong Kong, Chew Keen was told all reservations to Canada were full. The Great War was entering its third year and many of the passenger ships had been outfitted for war. They had to wait for availability. The wait stretched from a few days to months.

During the wait, Mon Ho stayed mostly indoors. "There were all sorts of strange men out there," Mon Ho told her daughter many years later. "I didn't feel comfortable being out by myself."

She worried about getting lost because she could not read the street signs. But what she feared most was to be harassed by men on the streets. The only time she would venture out was with her husband. This did not happen very often; Chew Keen was occupied in meetings with his relatives and business associates in Hong Kong.

He continued to work on the new village plans and rally support from relatives abroad. Responses were slow but some finally came through. The issue of family safety remained his main concern. Before he left China, the country had already plunged into a state of fighting among warlords for territories and power. Amid the chaos, law and order collapsed and banditry rampaged throughout the country. The lawless society worried everyone inside and outside of China.

Chew Keen's long stay in Hong Kong gave him an opportunity to meet with Dah Seen who happened to be in town. Acting as a liaison between Chew Keen and his family in China, Dah Seen was also a Gum San man in Australia who operated a trading company in Philip Bay near Melbourne as well as in Hong Kong. Throughout their regular correspondence, Dah Seen addressed Chew Keen as "uncle" though they were close in age. Whether they had a real relationship as uncle and nephew remains unknown because of the incomplete lineage pedigree.

Chew Keen and Dah Seen discussed the village ordeal and the unrest in China. Since they left their families behind in Dong Oin Lei, both shared the same concern about the safety of their loved ones. As Dah Seen often travelled for his business between Hong Kong and Australia, and sometimes to China, he was in a better position to monitor the situation. Chew Keen entrusted his family to his "nephew" if anything should happen. Together, they made an emergency plan, hoping it would not be carried out.

After a three-month stay in Hong Kong, on July 5, 1917, Chew Keen and Mon Ho finally embarked on the *S.S. Empress of Russia*, an ocean liner much bigger than the one Chew Keen took when he first crossed the Pacific. Apparently, no steerage tickets were available; they were lucky to secure the third-class cabin tickets. But even in these better conditions, Mon Ho still got seasick when the ship started rolling. The long voyage had just begun.

There were only thirty Chinese passengers on board and many of them were returning merchants, labourers or students. Six of them were female, including Mon Ho. Compared to the number of Chinese immigrants in the last century, the number had declined greatly because of the high entrance fees imposed by the Canadian government. Before boarding the ship, the captain collected five hundred dollars from each new Chinese immigrant. The passenger list recorded Mon Ho's fee payment.

Departing from Hong Kong, the ocean liner sailed north along the east coast of China and called in at the Port of Tsingtao, a major eastern seaport located in the Shandong Peninsula. Like Hong Kong, Tsingtao was a treaty port but it was occupied by Imperial Germany since 1898. After the outbreak of the Great War in 1914, Imperial Japan took it over from German hands. The ship docked long enough to let 2,299 Chinese coolies on board. They were kept in steerage below deck away from the rest of the regular passengers.

The Chinese coolies belonged to the British Chinese Labour Corps on their way to France by way of the Canadian Pacific Railway—part of a secret operation by the Canadian government, which the media and Canadian public were not privy to at the time. The secret operation permitted 120,000 Chinese coolies to be shipped to the French front through Canada. Between the months of April and October in 1917, transpacific steamers were requested to free space for the transport of these men. This operation was one of the main reasons why Chew Keen had such a hard time reserving berths for their passage.

All the coolies were recruited from Shandong Province. They were first shipped across the Pacific to William Head on Vancouver Island and then transported in cattle cars by rail across Canada to the east coast where they boarded ships to France. They served as non-military personnel, who relieved allied troops fighting at the front from manual labour. They dug trenches, filled sandbags, unloaded ships, repaired roads and removed dead bodies. The labour corps was the Chinese participation in the Great War.

On July 23, 1917, after eighteen days of sailing on the ocean, Mon Ho set foot on Canadian soil for the first time. Her port of entry was Vancouver, known to Sze Yup people as *ham sui fau* 'saltwater city' (咸水埠). At the immigration office, for some reason, the five hundred dollar entrance fee was returned to Mon Ho, as her registration form was marked "Exempt" in the fee column. Perhaps, she was a wife of a naturalized British citizen. They stayed in Vancouver Chinatown for a couple of days before heading north.

Vancouver Chinatown had surpassed Victoria Chinatown in size when Mon Ho arrived. With a population of 3,600 Chinese residents, the town covered four city blocks. The infamous Canton Alley and Shanghai Alley were the centre of town surrounded by general merchandise stores, tailor shops, laundries and restaurants.

In Chinatown, Mon Ho probably felt like she was at home—people spoke her dialect and ate the food she liked. She might have noticed there were not many women. An obvious demographic fact in Chinatown was that the number of men greatly outnumbered women. With Chew Keen by her side, she felt safe and assured. The layover in Vancouver gave Mon Ho a moment to catch her breath before heading for North Cariboo, which was a three-day stagecoach ride on the Cariboo Wagon Road.

In 1917 the Pacific Great Eastern Railway (dubbed the "from nowhere to nowhere" railway) had not yet reached Quesnel. The Cariboo Wagon Road was the only way to get to the north from Vancouver. Chew Keen and Mon Ho took a train from Vancouver to Ashcroft where they could catch Barnard's Express stagecoach.

Back then the stagecoach on the Cariboo Wagon Road was not a scenic Sunday ride. Pulled by six horses, Mon Ho would have felt sudden leaps and jolts whenever the stagecoach started. Even after the horses settled into a trot, she would feel her joints jarred from the rattle of the wheels as the stagecoach went up the hills, around the sharp curves and over numerous bumps in the road.

Along the wagon road, there were no towns or villages, only roadhouses and horse stables. The road was leading into endless craggy mountains shrouded by tall trees and thick woods. Sometimes, the road itself was carved out from the big rocks. Mon Ho had lived all her life in a flat river delta where the land barely rose. Her travels took her deep into dark mountains where the land emptied itself of people. She might have begun to wonder if she could ever find her way home.

Finally, the express stagecoach pulled up in front of the Wah Lee store. Chew Keen and Mon Ho got off and were greeted by C.S. Wing and other store staff. The *Cariboo Observer* even put a few welcoming words in the paper on August 4:

> *C. Keen, of the Wah Lee Co., who has spent the past year or so in China returned to town Thursday afternoon, accompanied by his wife.*

At last, Mon Ho arrived in Quesnel, or *mou see* (茂士) as Chew Keen told her. A brief description of this gold mountain in 1918 can be found in *the Wrigley's British Columbia Directory*:

> *A post office and town on the Cariboo Road, 220 miles north of Ashcroft on the C.P.R. Railway, and 100 miles south of Prince George on the G.T.P. Railway. It is served by stage from both points by the Cariboo auto road and by local Fraser River steamers. Population: 500. Local resources: mining and mixed farming.*

From July 5 to August 2, Mon Ho had been travelling for nearly a month – first by ocean voyage, then a train ride and finally a stagecoach. The entire journey would have been extremely demanding, both physically and mentally, as she constantly processed new experiences. Soon after Mon Ho settled in, Chew Keen went back to work in his store and Mon Ho was left alone in the house.

From the moment she stole a glimpse of her future husband until she arrived in the middle of Gum San, a year had gone by. Mon Ho did not have any time to stop to think. Now, she began to take stock of her surroundings.

She was far away from everyone she knew—her mother, her sisters, her girlfriends and her hometown. She saw no gold in these big mountains. In Quesnel, she met a few married men without their families. She did not see any Chinese women. As a new bride and wife of a merchant, it was improper for her to go out and socialize with other men. Contrary to the luxurious life in Gum San that she had imagined, the reality of living in a remote, godforsaken place finally hit home.

Many years later, Mon Ho told her granddaughter, Sharon, "When I first came here, I cried and cried." She might have found comfort in her lament as many Sze Yup women did when they felt sad and alone. In her lament, she might have called out to her mother and her sisters that she missed them very much. In her own singing, she might have told them she saw no gold in Gum San, just a lonely life ahead. She wished they were close so that she could reach out to them.

New life in the Cariboo

At the age of forty-two, Chew Keen had a home of his own in Gum San. With his wife, Mon Ho, by his side, his communal bachelor life came to an end. He moved out of the room above the Wah Lee store and into the log house that he had bought a few years before. He lived the life of a married man—going to work in the store and returning home at the end of the day. His wife was there to share with him everything - meals, news and chitchats.

During the time when Chew Keen was in China, Quesnel's business community suffered a great loss. In January 1916, a huge fire engulfed eleven buildings. Most of them were business establishments, including two hotels, two general stores, a barbershop, the meat market, the Bank of British North America and two warehouses. The total loss reached $250,000. The Wah Lee store lost some inventory in one of the destroyed warehouses. By the time Chew Keen came back from China, everything was up and running again. Still, business was slow and hampered by the Great War.

Chew Keen, ca.1918. (Courtesy of the family)

News from Hong Kong was not cheerful either. Due to the ongoing war, the price of gold fell and the stock market plunged; money Chew Keen sent home dropped in value. Other disturbing news was reports of banditry in the Sze Yup region, which escalated out of control. Chew Keen must have kept such distressing news from Mon Ho, who was still adjusting to her life in Gum San.

One noticeable adjustment for Mon Ho would have been the long daylight in summer. In the Cariboo, the northern sun in August hung in the sky much longer than at home. If working from sunrise to sunset as she was taught since childhood, Mon Ho would not have had much time to sleep. The hot, dry Cariboo summer, however, would have been a welcome surprise, as Mon Ho was used to the tropical heat and humidity in Southern China.

As far as housekeeping went, daily chores in Gum San were not much different from those in her home village, except some new techniques involved such as getting water from the water pump, cooking meals on the cast iron stove instead of a big wok, or keeping the log house warm and ventilated in winter. One precaution could not be emphasized enough —fire prevention in a log house. Gradually, Mon Ho settled into her new home in Gum San. Before long, she learned she was not the only Chinese woman in town.

Two months before Mon Ho's arrival, C.D. Hoy, another Chinese merchant in Quesnel, brought his wife over from Hoi Ping County, one of the counties in the Sze Yup region. Her name was Lim Foon Hai. They lived right downtown, close to the Wah Lee store. C.D. Hoy's given name was Chew Dong Hoy (周东海) and his courtesy name was Chew Cong Won (周宗煦). He came to Canada in 1903 and was a jack-of-all-trades in the Cariboo region until 1913 when he bought a store in Quesnel from one of his relatives and established himself as a merchant.

Knowing another Chinese family in town, especially a woman who was in a similar situation as hers, Mon Ho must have felt Gum San would not be such a dismal place after all. When Mon Ho first met her new friend, Foon Hai was pregnant with her first child. The two women must have been glad that they were able to talk to each other in their own dialect and share their experience of living in Gum San and concern of becoming a mother in a strange land.

As the months went by, Mon Ho established her own rhythm in North Cariboo with the waning summer daylight. Before the first snowflakes touched the ground, Mon Ho learned she was pregnant with her first child. The news of Mon Ho's pregnancy coincided with the birth of Chew Keen's third son. Dah Seen informed Chew Keen that his first wife gave birth to a son and everything went well. Chew Keen named the newborn son Lung Jet (龙爵). With three sons and a daughter plus another one on the way, Chew Keen was a happy man.

Mon Ho, on the other hand, was worried. Without a wise old woman present to guide her and help with her pregnancy and childbirth, she would have to handle the birth on her own. At the age of eighteen, she was going to become a first-time mother in a completely strange place. Besides assurances from Dr. Baker, Mon Ho still followed the traditional Chinese protocol of "do's and don'ts" that had been passed down for generations.

The high rate of infantile death in old China created many wild tales and taboos that shrouded childbirth and mother-hood. The first month after delivery was called *choi yueh* 'sitting month' (坐月). The mother would be free from her household chores and allowed to rest in bed and look after her newborn.

Many beliefs and taboos dictated what the mother should eat and do during that month. Typical taboos included no baths or showers, no hair washing, no cold water and no outings at all. She would be put on a postnatal therapeutic food diet that was thought to help healing and recovery from childbirth. In the Sze Yup region, such food as *jue gueh chou* 'pork knuckles and ginger stew' (猪脚醋) and *guy due* 'wine chicken' (鸡酒) were among the must-have foods on the new mother's diet for a while.

The traditional pork knuckles and ginger stew was the most popular postnatal food in the Pearl River Delta. The stew contained ingredients such as pork knuckles, fresh ginger and eggs in their shell, which were cooked in sweet black rice vinegar in a tall clay pot with a glazed interior. It was believed that calcium from the pork bones and eggshell dissolved in the vinegar through the cooking process. This would help the mother replenish the loss of calcium during pregnancy. Ginger would help lactation, and protein-rich eggs would help repair muscles. Wine chicken was another dish prepared with Chinese herbs, wood fungus and peanuts, and cooked with rice wine. It was said to have a similar therapeutic effect.

The cooking process usually began weeks before the due date. Some of the food was made beforehand; other food was prepared daily. An extra pair of hands was helpful and an elderly woman would be ideal. In Gum San, if her husband did not help, Mon Ho would have to do it by herself. Luckily, not only could Chew Keen cook the meals, with his Chinese herbal knowledge, he could also prepare what was good for her.

Mon Ho spent her first Cariboo winter preparing for the birth of her first baby and sharing this experience with her friend, Foon Hai. A few months after Foon Hai giving birth to a girl, Mon Ho also gave birth to a healthy baby girl. She was born on June 18, 1918 in the log house with Dr. Baker in attendance. The girl's birth was announced in the *Cariboo Observer*. Following Chinese custom, Chew Keen named her Kin Ying (琼瑛) when she was three months old. Mon Ho called her Ah Ying.

Mon Ho with her first child, Kin Ying in 1918.
Photo by C. D. Hoy (Courtesy of the family)

Chew Keen, Mon Ho and baby Kin Ying
in front of the log house on Reid Street North, Quesnel, 1918.
Photo by C. D. Hoy (Courtesy of the family)

The births of two Chinese babies brought some novelty and excitement to the small Chinese community that was mostly made up of "bachelors". They gave the Chinese residents reason to celebrate the occasion with special food—pork knuckles and ginger stew. For the following ten years, residents of Quesnel would continue to smell vinegar and wine on the breeze as it wafted from the chimneys of the Keens and the Hoys.

With the arrival of her first baby, Mon Ho was preoccupied by the routines of a new mother—feeding the baby, changing and washing diapers, and maintaining the household. The baby gave Mon Ho the hope and strength needed to have a life in Gum San. She was not aware that her husband was troubled by a hostage crisis in his home village, Dong Oin Lei.

Raid in Dong Oin Lei

Shortly after Chew Keen returned to Quesnel, letters followed him from Hong Kong and Australia by the Royal Mail steamers and Canada Post. The postal service had improved considerably since Wah Lee's time. In the early twentieth century, letter correspondence was more frequent and regular between the continents, but it was non-existent in rural China. Very often, Hong Kong became the place to relay messages between China and overseas.

Chew Keen must have valued every letter from home so much that he pasted them together for a keepsake. Unlike the remittance letters, which were more businesslike, the letters to Chew Keen were personal. First, they confirmed reception of money sent by Chew Keen, and then they informed about what was happening at home and in the village. Sometimes they commented on some local issues, other times gossiping with humour.

The first few letters in his collection came from his relatives in Australia, showing their support for the new village plan and their pledges for the new houses. It looked like construction was imminent. When 1918 came along, however, the ambitious plan was postponed because of the impact of the Great War. The tone of the letters became cautious and troublesome.

The villagers in Dong Oin Lei were scared to venture out after dark. More and more robberies occurred in the woods and in the graveyards. Bandits tended to come out and raid villages at night. In Da Zap Township, a retired militiaman was called to lead a security squad that would patrol the neighbouring area. The villages within the patrolling area sent their men to join the squad or donated money to arm them.

Unfortunately, Dong Oin Lei was outside the patrol boundary and left to its own defenses. Chew Keen realized the seriousness of the situation. All he could do from afar was monitor the situation. Perhaps, one small reassurance for him was the thought that his cousin and business partner, C.S. Wing, was in China visiting his own family during that time. Soon after Chew Keen's return with Mon Ho, C.S. Wing decided to pay a family visit at the end of 1917. He must have kept Chew Keen informed with firsthand accounts of the situation at home.

One month before Mon Ho gave birth, Chew Keen received letters from his relatives informing him that Gou Zan (高撰), one of Chew Keen's relatives and a close personal contact in Hong Kong, was gunned down during a raid in Dong Oin Lei.

The raid took place on April 18, 1918. At ten o'clock that night when the villagers retired for the evening, a gang of armed bandits stormed the village. They broke into the homes demanding money with threats to take the children away if their demand was not met. Gou Zan, who worked in Hong Kong, happened to be in the village visiting his family. He tried to intervene when the bandits tried to take his two young nephews away. The bandits shot him dead on the spot and took away sixteen young men and women from the village as hostages for ransom. Such detailed information did not reach Chew Keen until mid-May.

"Your family escaped the ordeal unharmed with only some valuables lost," it said in one letter. "Right now Dah Seen is helping them move out of the village. They are staying in Sun-wui town where they will be safe for the time being."

Then a letter from Dah Seen himself gave a full report. He told Chew Keen,

... Bandits raided the entire village and took sixteen men and women as hostages. One of them is your niece. By the grace of our ancestors, your family and my family are safe and unharmed. Everyone is terrified. I have removed them from the village. ... Remember what we have discussed when we last met in Hong Kong? So, I would like to take the liberty to ask our friend to find a rental house for both of our families until things calm down. They are temporarily staying with our good friend, Ou Gut Sun (区吉臣) in Sun-wui town. Meanwhile I am looking for a place for them. As you know, the move and rental will result in some extra cost.

Letter to Chew Keen reporting the raid on the village.

Chew Keen was not completely surprised by news of the raid. He was shocked, however, at the death of Gou Zan and the large number of hostages taken. The bandits targeted Dong Oin Lei for the obvious reason – ransom. The bandits did not take the old or little children, but young people. They demanded a lump sum of ¥3000 plus ¥500 for each hostage. Every time money was sent to release a hostage, the bandits would demand an additional release fee of ¥200.

At first, the villagers were in shock and disbelief. Families affected by the hostage taking pleaded for help from their overseas relatives. Then, they became so angry at the unreasonably high ransom that they talked about raising funds to buy weapons. One of the letters from Australia expresses their alarm:

> *...Urgent! After reading this letter, please send money home to help your family. The elders in the village have discussed how to raise money to buy arms and protect the lives and properties of the villagers. We have raised 450 pounds and will send it to Hong Kong where Gou Dye (高弟) can purchase the guns. ... Some of the villagers in Dong Oin Lei are talking about building a watchtower if we get enough money.*

Gou Dye (高弟) was C.S. Wing's courtesy name. When the hostage crisis took place in Dong Oin Lei, he was in his village nearby. The raid had a rippling effect on other villages, especially in those with a sizeable number of Gum San men. C.S. Wing moved his family to the town of Kongmoon for the time being.

The hostage negotiation took five to six months. A large sum of money was paid before all the hostages were released. The whole ordeal marked the beginning of a troublesome time that put Chew Keen and many overseas Chinese on high alert. Many of them began sending money home to build fortified houses. Some tried to get young people out of China. In one letter to Chew Keen, Dah Seen wrote,

> *After the kidnapping, our young men want to leave, anywhere abroad. ... One of the places is Cuba. There are not many seats on the ships to Cuba. Once they are on sale, they are gone in a few hours. So sad to see that happens nowadays.*

The immigration door had been shut to Chinese immigrants in the United States and Australia, and the door to Canada was also closing. A few decades before, Cuba had been a place for coolies. Now it was a sought-after destination.

By the end of 1918, after the situation calmed down, Chew Keen's wives and children moved back to Dong Oin Lei. Everyone tried to return to normalcy. Chew Keen's niece, who had been released from the hostage taking, finally got married. As her uncle and guardian, Chew Keen would have to pay for her dowry, in addition to a pair of gold earrings and a pair of gold bracelets with a dragon-phoenix design. The tone of letters from home returned to the mundane practicality of business and anecdotes.

On November 11, 1918, the Great War finally came to an end, and everyone looked to the future. In February 1919, C.S. Wing returned from China with his second bride, Yip Shee, an eighteen-year-old girl from Kongmoon, the same district Mon Ho came from. The Chinese family community was expanding with the arrival of another bride.

The Keen house on the 200 Block on Reid Street, ca. 1928.
(Courtesy of the family)

EIGHT
FAMILY LIFE IN QUESNEL (1917–1928)

There were only five Chinese families in Quesnel and vicinity at the beginning of the 1920s. Besides the Keens, Wings, and Hoys were two other families, the Lees and the Sings. They were farmers living in their ranches outside the Quesnel town site. Chan Sing Lee lived in the Marguerite area on the west bank of the Fraser River downstream from Quesnel. The well-known Nam Sing family lived on the east bank of the Fraser River, five miles upstream.

Nam Sing was one of the earliest Chinese miners to arrive in Quesnel from California in 1859. He was the first Chinese farmer in the Quesnel area and sold his fresh produce to Barkerville miners as early as 1867. In 1880 he brought his wife from China and together they raised their family on the Nam Sing Ranch. It is said that Nam Sing's wife never stepped off the farm her entire life after her arrival in the Cariboo.

The other three Chinese families in town were merchants. The town newspaper would often address the heads of these families with their business names, such as C. Keen of Wah Lee store. Their wives became "Mrs." in conjunction with their husbands' names, which made the women feel accepted and proud.

The common title "Mrs." was their closest connection with western culture. These women did not learn English beyond a few phrases of daily greetings. Most of the time, they stayed home, raising children and socializing among themselves. Being young and adaptable, they soon called Quesnel home while trying to keep true to the Chinese traditions and custom. The 1920s was a time for them to learn and grow while their husbands were busy trying to revive their suffering businesses after the Great War.

Chinese community in Quesnel

Clustered on Barlow Avenue between Front Street and Reid Street were a few Chinese-owned stores and cabins. The local residents referred to it as "Chinatown," but it was in fact too small to be a town. In Wah Lee's time, Quesnel, as a miners' winter "retreat", might have had a Chinatown, complete with a Chinese Masonic Hall and other association buildings such as Gee Gong Tong, Kong Soong Tong and Oylin society. The Chinese would have hosted gatherings and celebrations in these places with roast pigs and firecrackers. As early as 1887, in the town's introduction, the Quesnel community made note of the Chinese presence and their contribution: "The Chinese on the bars of both rivers contribute to swell the revenue of the place."

Since then, the Chinese community was shrinking in size as Chinese miners and labourers returned to their homeland or moved away to the coast. The abandoned Chinese Masonic Hall on the corner of Barlow Avenue and Front Street was deemed unsafe and torn down in early 1914. The other society buildings were left unoccupied. The population of Chinese residents in Quesnel dwindled to a couple dozen men. Among them were owners and workers in the Chinese business establishments.

In the 1920s, there were five general stores in Quesnel—John A. Fraser, Wah Lee, Yan War, S.N. Williams and C.D. Hoy—four owned by Chinese. The Wah Lee store was one of the oldest

Chinese general stores in Quesnel; another old Chinese store was Yan War (人和), which sold Chinese herbs and traded esoteric ingredients such as owls, deer horns and bear paws. Besides merchandising, trading gold and furs was a major part of the business in Chinese-owned general stores.

Other Chinese-owned businesses included Won Kee Laundry & Bakery and small shops in between such as C.H. Davie Watches Cleaned & Repaired Shop, Choo's Harness and Repair Shop, and C.C. Tom's Repair Shop. The initial "C" that often appeared in the names of the Chinese residents or businesses drew the attention of local residents, who assumed the "C" stood for *Charlie*. Actually, with a couple of exceptions, the letter "C" stood for the family name Chew (周).

The owner of Won Kee Laundry & Bakery was from a Chan (陈) clan. He later sponsored one of his relatives, Willie Fun (Chan Hie Foun) to come to Quesnel in 1913. Willie later became one of the owners of Quesnel's famous restaurant, the Nugget Café. Another Chinese businessman who was not from the Chew clan was Wong Ming Chow. He belonged to a Wong (黄) clan.

Whether they were clans of the Chews or Chans or Wongs, they all came from the Sze Yup region, mostly from Hoi-ping County, except for the Keens and Wings who came from Sun-wui County. Conveniently, they all spoke the same dialect, Sze Yup.

Their English surnames, Keen, Wing, Hoy, Fun, Sing and Lee, were actually part of their given names in Chinese. The mix-up arose from a reversal of naming conventions. Whereas in an English name, the first word is a given name and the last word a surname, the opposite is true in Chinese. For reasons still not clear to us today, the Chinese residents of Quesnel kept their adopted English surnames and eventually passed them down to their children. The names in Chinese have their own meaning:

Keen	坚	'strong or resolute'
Wing	榮	'glory or prosper'
Hoy	海	'ocean or sea'
Fun	辉	'rightness or brilliance'
Sing	星	'star or spark'
Lee	利	'advantage or profit'

After the Great War, the tiny Chinese business community looked to a better future. In its season's greetings advertisement on Dec 27, 1919, the Wah Lee store extended its good wishes to the Quesnel residents: "The war is over, the railway is coming to town, and good times are at hand for everyone."

Just as the roaring twenties rolled into big urban centres with more affordable automobiles, bobbed haircuts, flapper dresses and jazz music playing on the gramophone, Quesnel finally got its long-promised wish: the much-anticipated construction of a train station that would bring the Pacific Great Eastern Railway from the coast to Quesnel. At the same time, a new bridge across the mighty Fraser River to connect West Quesnel was in the planning stage.

The year 1920 looked prosperous, as indicated by the opening of three Chinese-owned restaurants in Quesnel—the Globe Café operated by the Wah Lee Company, the Good Eat Café owned by S.N. Williams & Co. and the Nugget Café co-owned by Won Kee, Willie Fun and Fook Gouie Chow. The Wah Lee store also installed an automatic gasoline-dispensing tank at the east side of the store on Reid Street. After trying to run the Globe Café for a few years, the Wah Lee Company sold the restaurant to another proprietor, Fook Chung.

After the completion of the railway in 1921, freight and passenger trains began running on a regular schedule. D.P. Lockhart, Secretary for the Board of Trade in Quesnel, painted an optimistic picture in 1923:

With the advent of railway transportation this country is now in a fair way to receive its merited attention. And it will be apparent to all that a district that has flourished for so many years without adequate means of transportation will, with transportation now at its gates, providing outside markets, etc., have a future which is full of potentialities, giving good security to the investor and prosperity to the settler.

The outlook for Chinese immigrants was not so optimistic in 1923. Since the five hundred dollar head tax was imposed on the Chinese, few new Chinese immigrants came to Canada and fewer to Quesnel. The Canadian immigration policy was making it harder for ordinary Chinese residents to bring their families over to Canada unless they were merchants or businessmen. The Chinese men continued to outnumber Chinese women in Canada during this time.

C.D. Hoy's family told how their father brought over his wife. He came to Canada in 1903 and worked a variety of jobs. In 1911 he went back to China to marry Foon Hai but returned without her because the five-hundred-dollar head tax was a lot of money at that time. He was determined to bring her over. For the next six years, he worked very hard and saved every penny. He bought a business from a relative and established himself as a merchant. In 1917 he went back to China again and finally brought Foon Hai over.

In Quesnel, only one more Chinese family with children joined the community in the 1920s; it was Wong Ming Chow's family. In November 1918 Chow William Suns, the former Chinese owner of S.N. Williams & Co. died of Spanish flu. Wong Ming Chow and Chew Sip Poy bought the store in 1920. After establishing himself as a businessman, Wong brought his wife Loo Sen and their two teenage sons from China in 1923 before the immigration door completely shut to Chinese immigrants.

In postwar Canada, the economic conditions were poor and Chinese immigrants were often blamed for taking work away from Canadians. On July 1, 1923, the *Chinese Immigration Act*, also known today as the *Chinese Exclusion Act*, took effect. It banned any new Chinese immigrant from entering Canada except diplomats, Canadian-born children, merchants and students. For the Chinese residents already in Canada, the act required:

> *...For each Chinese immigrant who has been per-*
> *mitted to land in or enter Canada a certificate*
> *containing a description and photograph of such*
> *individual, the date of his arrival and the name*
> *of the port of his landing, and such certificate*
> *shall be **prima facie** evidence that the person*
> *presenting it has complied with the requirements*
> *of this Act;...*

Within twelve months after coming into effect, the Chinese community had to comply. Every Chinese born in Canada was required to carry an immigration I.D. card.

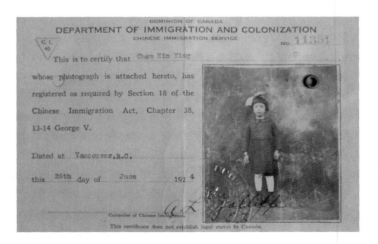

Kin Ying's I.D. card. (Courtesy of the family)

Although the Chinese residents in Quesnel were far away from the major Chinese communities such as Vancouver and Victoria, they were well informed from newspapers of what was going on beyond the mountains of the Cariboo. The Wah Lee store became a place for the Chinese residents to collect their mail, ask for news from home and read Chinese newspapers from Vancouver and Hong Kong. Wah Lee & Co. subscribed to a few Chinese language newspapers, including the *Chinese Times* (大汉公报) from Vancouver, *Chung Sai Yat Po* 'China West Daily' (中西日报) from San Francisco and two other newspapers from Hong Kong, *Universal Circulating Herald* (循环日报) and *China Mail* (华字日报). The newspaper subscription was essentially a free service for the good of the Chinese community. Everyone was welcome to the newspapers in the store.

Like English newspapers, Chinese newspapers covered news stories in China and the world. They usually provided the information that had a direct impact on Chinese immigrants in Canada and immigration policies in other countries. Though the overseas Chinese were far away from China, they were still concerned about what was going on in their homeland and how it would affect their families. The newspapers broke the social isolation and helped the Quesnel Chinese community connect with the world, at least with Vancouver Chinatown. Sometimes there was more than news and editorial in the papers, something entertaining such as short stories, humour and travel journals.

As an educated man, Chew Keen enjoyed reading the newspapers very much, not only for the purpose of information, but also for the literary value. He did not want good stories to go to the wastebasket, so he would cut out the entertainment section from the old newspapers and bound them together for his later enjoyment. Today, the Keen family still keeps two thick volumes of his newspaper cut outs that dates back from the 1920s.

In 1925 Quesnel's Chinatown got even smaller after the "Chinatown Fire." One night in June, a lamp was accidentally knocked over in one of the rooms upstairs in the Good Eat Café, igniting a blaze that burned down the building and quickly spread to other buildings. Two people died in the fire. The affected businesses included the Good Eats Café, S.N. Williams store, Won Kee's Laundry, C.C. Tom Repairs, Choo's Harness Repairs, C.H. Davie Watch & Jewellery and the Nugget Café. Miraculously, the Wah Lee store on the south side of Barlow Avenue escaped the fire.

Some of the burned-down buildings were unoccupied cabins including a vacant Chinese association building, which were not rebuilt after the fire. Otherwise, the Chinese business venues were rebuilt as quickly as possible. A week after the fire, the *Cariboo Observer* reported: "The Nugget Café expects to open for business on Thursday next, in the Globe building, immediately opposite their former premises next to the Wah Lee store." The Nugget Café in the new location now had five partners—Won Kee, Willie Fun, Shee Chow, Nam Chow and Fook Gouie Chow. With new business and development opportunities, the 1920s was an exciting era for the men in the Chinese business community. Meanwhile, their wives had to keep up with the accelerating pace of life. For the next ten years or so, the number of Chinese residents in Quesnel increased as many babies were born to the Keens, the Hoys and the Wings. The three women managed to keep Doctor Baker on his toes.

Life in the Keen house

After Kin Ying, five more children were born in the Keen's log house on the 500 block of Reid Street North. Lung Fee (龙辉) was born in 1920; Kin Boyd (琼佩) in 1921 and, in May 1922, a baby boy was born but died a few days later from unknown causes. In the spring of 1923, Lung Bew (龙標) was born and, in 1925, Lung Chick (龙卓). After eight years in Gum San, twenty-five-year-old

Mon Ho had become the mother of five children; the oldest was only seven years old.

Mon Ho with her four children, 1924. (Left to right): Kin Boyd (aged 3 yrs), Kin Ying (aged 6 yrs), Lung Bew (aged 1yr) and Lung Fee (aged 4yrs).
(Courtesy of the family)

In keeping with the Chinese heritage, Chew Keen gave Chinese names to all the children born in Canada consistent with those in China. The given names of his sons, six of them, shared one character Lung 'dragon' (龙) while the daughters had the character Kin 'elegant' (琼). Not forgetting the family name, he also incorporated the family name "Chew" into the names of his Canadian-born children—Kin Ying Chew Keen, Lung Fee Chew Keen, Kin Boyd Chew Keen, Lung Bew Chew Keen and Lung Chick Chew Keen. For whatever reason, Chew Keen's Canadian-born sons were not given courtesy names, unlike his Chinese-born sons who had their courtesy names with the generation character Dah (达).

The log house was getting too small for the growing family. In December 1922, Mr. Kenny Mackenzie, the town contractor was called to construct an additional room on the north side of the house. Only a few years later, Chew Keen began looking for a bigger house for his family of seven. He bought the Duclos cottage next to the Wah Lee store in 1926.

The Duclos cottage was located on the 200 block of Reid Street opposite the *Cariboo Observer* office, one block from the public school. Its proximity to everything saved the children trekking long distances through the snow for school in winter. In the spring of 1928, Chew Keen had some renovations done with a new picket fence built along the front of the property and a new walkway around the house. He also hired P. McLean to re-shingle the roof.

The grey-and-white wooden frame cottage with a fully enclosed lean-to was not a big house but modest and functional for a large family. A short path from Reid Street led past lilac bushes to a front porch. A small front room was the entrance that connected the main floor and the lean-to where the family kitchen was. Straight ahead from the front room was a staircase that led to the attic where two bedrooms were for the children, one for the girls and the other for the boys. The parents' bedroom was on the main floor adjoining the back of the living room. Both living room and kitchen had big windows facing Reid Street.

As a merchant of a general merchandise store, the family could have shipped in luxury household furniture such as solid brass beds, cushioned couches or modern refrigerators. Instead, the Keen's household furniture was all made of wood—simple, practical, functional and economical, reflecting traditional Chinese values.

In the living room stood a cast-iron wood-burning stove by a brick chimney wall; it was mainly used for winter heating. A few chairs were placed around the room for guests. In one corner of the living room sat the Keen's first home appliance—a foot treadle sewing machine that Mon Ho used to make clothes for the family.

In the 1920s, electric lighting for households depended on individual gas powered generators that made an awful noise. Thanks to the Cariboo Hotel that had its own power plant, lighting at the Keen house was connected to the hotel's power line, which kept the house relatively quiet. Every night at eleven o'clock, the lights would flash three times before the power generator was shut down, preparing the residents for a quiet night of rest.

The kitchen was the centre of family life. A big wood-burning stove with double burners dominated the room as cooking space. Mon Ho always kept a very big pot of water on one of the burners. This was essential for cooking and washing in the winter when the water pipes froze during cold snaps. Another big piece of furniture was the kitchen table where the family gathered for meals, children did their schoolwork and Mon Ho cut out sewing patterns. To protect the table and make it easy to clean, Mon Ho covered it with a piece of oilcloth.

At the end of the kitchen was a small, narrow back room that served as the family's washing and storage space. Inside, there was a small cupboard to keep all the dishes, bowls and chopsticks. A big sink occupied most of this room serving as the family washing station—after all, those were the days of no indoor plumbing. The sink took care of the family's cleaning needs, such as washing up in the morning, preparing daily meals, taking a sponge bath in winter. Mon Ho kept a few enamel basins handy for different purposes as the day progressed. Family laundry of seven was done on the back porch.

The uncovered back porch was made of wooden planks that ran along the back wall of the house. Conveniently, the kitchen side door opened to the back porch where Mon Ho stored her food in a screened cupboard. When Chew Keen had time, he made tofu for the family on the back porch. The Keen children used to gather around watching their father grind the fully soaked soybeans into soymilk with a pair of stone mills, which must have been shipped from China. After the soymilk was boiled, coagulated and pressed, there would be delicious and fresh homemade tofu for dinner that day. "Dad sometimes made some delicious desert tofu, too." Beatrice remembered fondly.

Off the back porch was Mon Ho's Chinese vegetable garden. She did not care much for the root vegetables popular in other households in Quesnel; she missed her Chinese vegetables. The Cariboo summer provided plenty of sunlight for growing green vegetables, often with good results. If there were a surplus of vegetables, Mon Ho would sun dry and store them for the winter.

Every year, in late April or early May when the soil was soft enough, she would begin to till it, piling it in rows and sowing the seeds as she used to do in the garden of her home village. Due to the short frost-free season, she tried a variety of fast-growing green Chinese vegetables such as *bok choi* 'Chinese cabbage' (白菜), *guy choi* 'mustard leaf' (芥菜) and *hoi lan duo* 'sweet peas' (荷兰豆). Guy Choi was a popular vegetable in Mon Ho's hometown, Kongmoon.

Using Chinese agricultural practices, Mon Ho would use diluted night soil or chicken manure for fertilizer. Like every other household in Quesnel, she also raised a few dozen chickens for eggs and meat. Half of the shed next to the house was cordoned off for the chicken coop. When the children were old enough, they lent a helping hand.

The boys used to split firewood on Saturdays to replenish the weekly supplies for heating and cooking while the girls helped with housekeeping and washing. But one chore none of them liked to do was gathering eggs from the chicken coop. The distinct and pungent odour of chicken manure seared the memory of the girls so that ninety years later they could still recall the awful smell. Nonetheless, everyone loved the steamed chicken dish their father made, especially the dipping sauce garnished with fresh minced green onions and ginger.

Living in the north, family health was Chew Keen's main concern. Tuberculosis was still rampant in the early twentieth century in the area; Chew Keen knew a few adults and children who had succumbed to the disease. The devastation of the Spanish flu epidemic after the Great War left a deep scar in the memory of the Quesnel residents. Chew Yon, a cook for the Wah Lee store, was the second local victim who lost his life to the flu.

For that very reason, Chew Keen could not let down his guard. He used his knowledge of Chinese herbal medicine to promote his family's health, often incorporating them into his cooking. Following each season, he would brew different types of Chinese herbal teas and require his children to drink up. The most potent herbal drink was the tonic juice from Korean ginseng.

Chinese belief in the tonic properties of ginseng has a long history. Its juice is believed to have powerful effects on boosting and supporting the immune system. Chew Keen made the juice the traditional way—dried ginseng root was sliced into small thin pieces, placed inside a small ceramic cup and filled with water to give the desired concentration. The cup had a double lid, a cone-shaped lid over a flat one inside. It was placed in a pot of hot water that would simmer for at least five hours until the dried ginseng in the cup became soft and tender. Alone, the ginseng juice tasted very bitter so Chew Keen used sweetened dried plums to entice his children to drink up their medicine. He used the same sweetening tactic to get the children to drink bitter herbal teas when they came down with a cold.

The Keen children lived a traditional Chinese way of life as they grew up. The first language they learned was Sze Yup dialect; Mon Ho sang them to sleep with folk songs in her native

Sze Yup. Outside their home, their playmates were the children of the Hoys and the Wings, who also spoke only Sze Yup. They often played together and watched out for each other just as in a Chinese village.

Raising five children without another pair of helping hands, Mon Ho had little free time for herself. Before she got married, she was a great fan of Cantonese opera, which originated from the Pearl River Delta and was very popular at the beginning of the twentieth century in the Sze Yup region. She must have been to the market fairs with her sisters or girlfriends and watched Cantonese opera performed on a makeshift stage. Since arriving in Quesnel, she was cut off from such live entertainment.

If she had lived in a bigger Chinese community, such as Chinatown in Victoria or Vancouver, Mon Ho might have had an opportunity to watch live performances. Cantonese opera was very popular among the overseas Chinese, and performing troops were often invited for tours overseas. But the Chinese community in Quesnel was too tiny and too remote. Mon Ho must have missed that very much.

Not until the late 1920s when ten-inch vinyl records of opera singing became available for home enjoyment, was she able to listen to Chinese opera records on a hand-winding gramophone and, in her own private moments, sing along. The gramophone was their first luxury item. By then, her children had already learned English in school and did not develop an appreciation for Cantonese opera. They preferred their local programs on the Spartan radio, broadcasting English tunes.

East meets West

Years flew by in a busy house full of children. In 1924 Mon Ho's oldest child, Kin Ying, reached school age. In British Columbia, all children six years of age were required by law to go to school. Back in rural China, a girl of six would be put in charge of her younger siblings or learn fancy needlework; school would not be part of her education. In Canada, all children, boys and girls, went to school.

In the past, Chinese immigrants would have preferred their Canadian-born sons to receive a Chinese education. In North Cariboo, other Chinese families had tried three different Chinese educational options over the years: sending them back to China the way C.S. Wing did, hiring a private Chinese tutor the way Nam Sing did on his farm or going to the Chinese Public School in Victoria Chinatown as Bill Hong did.

By the 1920s, however, these educational options were impractical and expensive. Chew Keen might not have considered any of these options at all. He must have realized the world had changed and an English education was not a bad idea for his Canadian-born children. Mon Ho would not have any objections; the opportunity to go to school was as good as gold.

In September of 1924, Kin Ying enrolled in the Quesnel Superior School, a one-room schoolhouse on the corner of Carson Avenue and McLean Street. At that time, the Keens still lived in the log house on the 500 block of Reid Street North, four blocks away from the school. The streets at that time were unpaved without sidewalks. Kin Ying did not remember how she got there, but she would not forget her first day in school.

The Quesnel Superior School in the 1920s.
All the Keen children started their education in this one-room school.
(Courtesy of the Quesnel Museum)

The children and teacher spoke English, and Kin Ying did not understand what was going on in the classroom. The experience could have been more traumatic for a little girl of six had her friend Avaline Hoy not been there with her. Avaline was in the same predicament. Both girls stuck close to each other, putting on a brave face. They soon found another Chinese girl, Laura Sing, Nam Sing's granddaughter, who was also attending her first day of school. Laura lived on the farm two miles north of Quesnel. Her father, Him Kong Sing, drove her to school in a horse and buggy.

For the entire first day of school, the three Chinese girls stayed close to each other. They did not understand a word the teacher said but watched the other children closely following what they did. From that day on, Kin Ying, Avaline and Laura became "chums," as Kin Ying called their friendship. Anxiety about school continued for a while until Kin Ying began to learn and speak English.

As the first child and the first girl in Chew Keen's family to go to an English school, Kin Ying was a pioneer in her own way who paved the way for her younger siblings. Lung Fee was the next to follow in his sister's footsteps.

Before Lung Fee went to school, Chew Keen decided to give his Canadian-born sons English names. He named them after his good friends. Lung Fee was named Charlie, after the town pharmacist, Charlie Allison. Lung Bew was named Billy, after the town barber, Billy Lamb. Lung Chick was named Harry, after the town carpenter and builder, Harry Joyce. However, the boys' English names were not legally changed until 1978. At home, both parents would still call them by their Chinese names: Ah Fee, Ah Bew and Ah Chick.

For whatever reason, the Keen girls did not receive English names until they finished school. As the tradition went, Chew Keen did not think it important whether the girls had Chinese names or English names because they were not going to hold an office or work independently. They would be married and follow the name of their husbands.

Giving the boys English names was not the only western custom they followed. Influenced by the new twenties' trend, Mon Ho cut her hair and wore it in a short bob. Gone was the coiled-hair bun at the back of her head, the traditional Chinese symbol of a married woman. The dark, loosely fitting long gowns that she wore when she first arrived were put away in her trunk. In a better-fitting silk satin blouse with high collars and matching mid-calf-length skirt, Mon Ho became a fashionable and self-assured merchant's wife.

In Mon Ho's opinion, dressing well reflected the presence of one's self-respect and good manners. As a talented seamstress, she began to experiment with western fashion trends. She copied patterns from Eaton or Simpsons' catalogues and made her own western-style clothes on her sewing machine.

She also sewed her children's clothes. The girls always wore dresses with matching hats, bows or scarves, and the boys always wore cords or denim pants with suspenders, shirts and black boots. Mon Ho's sense of fashion was passed down to her children who always took care to dress their best according to the occasion.

Her husband, on the other hand, was a bit slower keeping up with the changing times. One incident became a family story. Dorothy Gardner, who was rather unconventional, was the only girl to wear jeans in a town where girls wore dresses. One day she rode to the Wah Lee store on horseback. Chew Keen looked down behind the counter and greeted her. "Now, what can I do for you, little boy?" he asked. Apparently, Dorothy took his remark in stride and carried on with her business.

Other western traditions began to find their way into the Keen house, starting with Santa Claus. Long before the children began to attend school, Chew Keen was aware about the Christmas holiday and often put out holiday greetings in the town newspaper on behalf of the Wah Lee store. The family, however, never celebrated the Christian holiday.

After Kin Ying went to school and learned about jolly Old Saint Nick, she came home and told her younger siblings the story of Santa. On Christmas Eve, Kin Ying and her siblings put up stockings by the stove in the living room before going to bed. The next morning, they were very excited to find each stocking stuffed with a mandarin orange, candies and assorted nuts in shells. They were further surprised by a fifty-cent coin inside their stockings. Hanging stockings by the fireplace on Christmas Eve became a tradition in the Keen house and Santa Claus never missed them on his delivery route.

Another big celebration was May Day, Queen Victoria's birthday; the holiday was celebrated in Quesnel Superior School. All the boys and girls dressed in their Sunday best for the special day. They would have a parade and be presented to a selected May Day "Queen." One time, Kin Ying and Willie Wing took part in the May Day parade, representing the Chinese nation. They dressed up in Chinese silk clothes and silk slippers. Mon Ho helped them make traditional headgear.

English school exposed the children not only to a world of ideas but also to the world of sports. Kin Ying learned all types of sports in school but enjoyed playing tennis the most. Before school, she would play a game or two on the tennis court with her classmates. Her younger sister Kin Boyd liked to play basketball, skate and ski. Such activities for girls were unthinkable in the old China, for this type of public exposure and physical exertion contradicted Confucian expectations of propriety, which strongly prohibited girls from running and jumping around in public.

The introduction of western culture and celebrations through school would not diminish the biggest celebration of the year in the Keen house—Chinese New Year. After the winter solstice, Chew Keen would send money to his family in China to help them buy all the special foods and new clothes for the celebration. He also ordered special foods from Vancouver for his family and the Chinese residents in Quesnel.

The Chinese in North Cariboo used to gather in Quesnel to celebrate the holiday. After the old Masonic hall was torn down and the association building burned down, the Wah Lee store would host one of the New Year's dinners for those Chinese who did not have families in town. Dishes like steamed chicken and roast pork were essential for the feast. After dinner, they played fan-tan games, dominoes and gambling games at the back of the store. The merriment would last for four days.

In the Keen house, Mon Ho would begin cleaning the house days before the celebration. Special decorations such as Chinese narcissus had to be shipped from Vancouver weeks before.

Mon Ho would plant the narcissus bulbs in a shallow bowl with water and pebbles. The narcissus blooms were symbols of luck and prosperity for the upcoming year. She would then prepare special Chinese pastries for the occasion.

The family's favourite pastries were *tia* (糕), *yo-zai-kok* (油炸角) and *jin-dui* (煎堆), which were made from rice flour filled with minced pork, sugar and peanuts, or nothing at all. Then, they were deep-fried in oil. Mon Ho's plain jin-dui was Chew Keen's favourite.

Traditionally, the most important dinner of the year was on Chinese New Year's Eve when every family member was present to celebrate the past year and welcome the new year. Each dish for the special dinner was full of symbolic good wishes—fish for abundance, oysters for good luck and hair moss fungi for prosperity. All day, Chew Keen and Mon Ho would be busy in the kitchen preparing these special dishes. Before dinner was served, Chew Keen and the boys would light firecrackers in the backyard.

On Chinese New Year's Day, Mon Ho would ask her children to deliver the homemade pastries to other Chinese residents in town, wishing them *gong hay fat choi* 'happy new year' (恭喜发财). In return, the Chinese residents would give the children *lai-see* 'good luck money' wrapped in small red envelopes. Imagine happy little Keens, Hoys and Wings running around town in the snow, delivering goodies. The noise of firecrackers and fireworks must have attracted the curiosity of the townspeople, or at very least the children.

The Chinese New Year's celebration later became such a big affair in Quesnel that the *Cariboo Observer* would post a notice about it, telling all the town residents of the upcoming event. The Chinese families would have an open house to welcome the residents, who could come and try out the special pastries, drink some Chinese rice wine and simply have a good time.

This generous invitation allowed Chew Keen's Canadian friends to share some joys of Chinese culture. It also provided an opportunity for the guests to learn that their host did not drink wine from a glass but only allowed himself to take alcoholic sips from a soup spoon. Chew Keen never strayed from this habit.

The residents in Quesnel regarded Chew Keen as an easy-going, tolerant and friendly merchant. They remember him smoking a two-foot-long bamboo water pipe. Every so often, children or a passer by would stop at the Wah Lee store to watch Chew Keen smoke tobacco with a strange instrument that made a gurgling noise when Chew Keen inhaled and exhaled.

Water pipe smoking, called hookah, originated in India centuries ago. Tobacco was first imported to China in the late sixteenth century along with water pipe smoking; it became very popular in Southern China. The Chinese used a bamboo pipe instead of an intricate glass pipe to hold the water, but the principle was the same—tobacco smoke passed through a water basin before inhalation. Chew Keen may have indulged in this pastime in China before coming to Canada.

As the head of the family, Chew Keen gained great respect from his children, not because he was the authority, but because he was a hardworking and reasonable man of few words. When he spoke, his words hung like pearls of wisdom. He often said to his children: "Be kind to others and respect the elders." The children learned at a very young age that there was no talking back to their parents and elders.

Another phrase that Chew Keen's daughter, Beatrice, remembers was "Let bygones be bygones." He had been through a lot in his life, carrying a heavy burden of responsibility and obligations. He did not like to hold grudges and encouraged his children to be forgiving to others. Chew Keen expected his children to do well in school. "Try your best and finish what you start with." When he learned that his daughter, Kin Ying, made the honour roll in grade five, he gave her a small diamond ring as a token of encouragement.

After Kin Ying, his other children entered the Quesnel Superior School one by one. Soon, English became a second language spoken in the house, especially in the children's bedrooms or among themselves outside the house. Out of respect to their parents, Sze Yup was still the first language spoken at home. Like many Chinese parents, Chew Keen was worried about his children's Chinese education, particularly the written language.

He used to be a teacher in his village school, so he decided to hold Chinese classes and teach his children after they finished English school. The Hoy girls came to join the Keens. The Chinese class was first held in the mezzanine of the Wah Lee store. The textbooks used for the lessons were classical Chinese texts such as *San Zi King* 'Three-Word Textbook' (三字经). Chew Keen also taught them how to write using a brush pen. Sometimes Mon Ho would come to join them during lesson time.

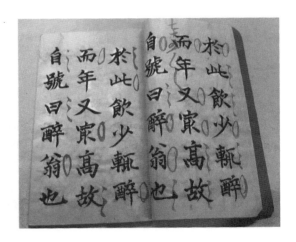

Harry's Chinese calligraphy practice book. Circular marks indicate good work.

(Photo by author)

Later the class was moved to the Hoy's old house, after the Hoy family moved into their new home. Then, Tom Owen Wong, a tailor and well-educated Chinese man from Edmonton, became their teacher. Since the Chinese lessons were piecemeal and inconsistent, the children didn't make much progress. The language required a lot of memory work and time to practice, and they were not interested in a language they could not relate to. They also found no purpose for it in an English-speaking country. To the children, China was a faraway foreign land beyond their reach.

Turmoil in China

In their father's mind, China was always present, not far away. Life in Dong Oin Lei had returned to normal after the traumatic hostage taking. Letters from Dah Seen were filled with anecdotes about market bazaars, the comings and goings of relatives, and special events such as the Hundred Sons Celebration in the clan temple. Chew Keen was glad that his mother was well and strong enough to travel to the market or pay a visit to the local temple. The families were in regular communication and sent pictures to each other.

In 1924 his oldest son, fourteen-year-old Lung Gong, was engaged to a girl from a Cheong family. Chew Keen must have felt some relief, for his first son was on the path of maturity and independence. Other news was also encouraging. The grain prices stabilized and Da Zap Township hosted a harvest celebration, engaging a Cantonese opera troupe for three days. In early 1925, Dah Seen's trading company in Australia expanded. Chew Keen was offered two shares in the new company, one in Chew Keen's name and the other in Mon Ho's name.

Chew Keen's two sons from his first wife, ca. 1924.
(Courtesy of the family)

But these good tidings were a deceptive calm before the storm. Away from the rural countryside, mostly in the north of China, a series of civil wars were raging on different fronts.

On the national front, Dr. Sun Yat-sen, the first president and founding father of the Republic of China, was leading a war to unify China and put an end to the warlord state. On the political front, tensions were heating up between the Kuomintang, the Chinese National Party, and the newly established Chinese Communist Party. In Kwangtung Province, the Kuomintang National Army and the Canton Merchant Volunteers Corps were fighting for economic control. As conflicts escalated into bloody battles, the general populace was caught in the middle.

Meanwhile, banditry continued unabated in the Sze Yup region. To safeguard their families against such turbulent times, many overseas Chinese invested their life savings to build watchtower-styled houses in their hometown, believing these tall structures would somehow protect their families.

In Dong Oin Lei, the proposal to build a watchtower was on the table. Before all parties reached consensus, a temporarily preventive measure was taken and they hired night watchmen for the village. Such payment for the hiring would come from the overseas Chinese expenditure account. In a letter to Chew Keen, Dah Seen explained the plan for the four-storey watchtower. It would serve as a lookout for any suspicious activities as well as a hiding place for the women and children in case of an attack. Each floor had a trap door to keep bandits out.

The villagers once again requested money from the overseas Chinese for the construction of the tower. In light of the last armed robbery, Chew Keen suggested the village purchase weapons from Canada. Dah Seen replied that the British colony had put a ban on imported weapons from other countries and that he would get them in Hong Kong.

Before completion of the watchtower, a general strike broke out in Kwangtung Province and Hong Kong. It was in response to a massacre in Canton, in which British troops opened fire into a group of Chinese demonstrators outside a British Concession. The strike called for the boycott of all British import and export goods, and roadblocks were set up prohibiting travel to Hong Kong from Mainland China.

From 1925 to 1926, the general strike held out for fourteen months. It devastated trade and paralyzed the economy in the British colony. A quarter million Chinese left Hong Kong for the mainland, leaving the bustling commercial island a ghost town. Dah Seen remained in Hong Kong; his letters to Chew Keen described the frustration and difficulty of exporting goods from

China. His firm paid high prices for the delay, resulting in a loss of profits.

In spite of the turmoil, Chew Keen's family in Dong Oin Lei carried on with life as normal as possible. In 1928 his oldest son, Lung Gong, got married at the age of eighteen before enrolling in Sun Yat-sen University in Canton. He was the first person in the family to go on to higher education. Chew Keen was very proud and supportive of his son's endeavour.

Unfortunately, Dah Seen, who helped purchase the engagement gifts from Hong Kong, was not able to attend Lung Gong's wedding. Before the watchtower was completed in 1926, Chew Keen received sad news from Dah Seen's son, informing him that Dah Seen had passed away unexpectedly during his family visit. For Chew Keen, this was a great loss of a dear friend and a close connection to his home village.

A family picture taken outside the Wah Lee store, ca.1930.
(Left to right): Kin Ying, Kin Boyd, Mon Ho, Chew Keen, Billy, Harry and Charlie.
(Courtesy of the family)

NINE
GROWING UP (1929–1938)

The roaring twenties brought the world a decade of high hopes and prosperity. In 1927 C.S. Wing, partner of the Wah Lee store, left the company and moved to Soda Creek with his family. He bought Louie & Co. store in Soda Creek from the owner, who had returned to China because of illness. The name Louie in Chinese was a family name (雷) meaning "thunder." For years the Wah Lee Company kept such a close business relationship with Louie & Co., that the locals thought it was part of the Wah Lee operation. However, they were "entirely separate and absolutely independent" from Wah Lee & Co.

Before C.S. Wing's departure for his new business venture, Chew Keen was the store accountant. When his partner went to Soda Creek, he took on the role of manager/accountant for the Wah Lee store. He remained a hard-working, modest and prudent Chinese merchant, who preferred working quietly behind the counter with his abacus.

In March of 1929, the Fraser River Footbridge was completed and opened to the public. The bridge spanned the mighty Fraser River from downtown Quesnel to West Quesnel, ending the dangerous river crossing by canoe and connecting the two communities. Quesnel was now a newly incorporated village and interconnected by three bridges: the Quesnel Bridge, the railway bridge and the new Fraser River Footbridge. With the bridges and the railway terminus at its doorstep, the village of Quesnel was ready to realize its potential.

Quesnel in 1930s. (Author's collection)

On Tuesday, October 30, 1929, investors around the world froze in horror as they watched the stock market plummet. The infamous Black Tuesday signalled the end of the roaring twenties and the start of a dismal era, the Great Depression, which spared no one in North America and many major nations around the world.

The Great Depression

When the year 1930 rolled in, there was no sign that the shroud of Black Tuesday would ever be lifted. Stock prices hit rock bottom, investments dried up and unemployment skyrocketed. Factories and offices shut down, putting massive numbers of people out in the streets. Long lines of hungry people queued up at the doorstep of every soup kitchen. There was so much despair that some Chinese immigrants left for China, or sent their family members back to home villages where they hoped their hard-earned money could be stretched a bit further.

China, in contrast, entered the Nanking Decade, also dubbed the Golden Decade, after the Kuomintang military defeated the warlords and unified China in 1928. Under the Kuomintang government led by Generalissimo Chiang Kai-shek, some law and order was restored, providing the country with a period of peace and stability.

In Kwangtung, the provincial government tried to promote and encourage overseas Chinese to invest in their homeland. In the Sze Yup region, new bridges and roads were built. A main road was constructed from Sun-wui to Hoi-ping, which ran past Da Zap Township and close to Dong Oin Lei. For the first time, overseas Chinese felt secure about investing money in their homeland.

Chew Keen became a grandfather in 1930. His oldest son, Lung Gong, had two boys, Yuk Tang and Fook Yum, who were born in Dong Oin Lei in 1930 and 1931, respectively. Their grandmother, Yu Shee, Chew Keen's first wife, helped look after the boys in the village while their father studied at university. Chew Keen's other young sons, Lung Shong and Lung Jet, were still in school. There was no mention in the family letters about his oldest daughter, Kin Bao, but according to her age and the custom of early marriage, she had likely married and moved to Malaya by then. Since Chew Keen returned to Canada, this was the first time the Chinese home front was calm and placid. Across the Pacific, however, the situation looked very different.

Before the Depression shock wave hit North Cariboo, business in Wah Lee & Co. prospered. The store was stocked with a wide range of merchandise from dried goods to hunting gear, household wares to hay, and grain to produce. A few local boys were hired to deliver goods and orders on bicycle. The store also bought a used 1923 Dodge truck for pick-ups and delivery.

As the Depression deepened, very little cash changed hands in the stores. A local barter system emerged in which customers traded their farm produce or eggs for daily necessities such as flour, sugar and tobacco. Trading was the core part of Wah Lee & Co.'s business; it used to do a lot of trading in gold and furs. During the Depression, every family was cash-strapped. Business in general was sluggish. The Quesnel Board of Trade asked the stores to close for a half-day on Thursdays.

At the beginning of 1933, the residents of Quesnel saw carloads of people turning up in town with their families. They came from drought-stricken Saskatchewan on their way to Wells, where there were job opportunities. Two gold quartz mining companies, the Cariboo Gold Quartz Mines and the Island Mountain Mines were in need of miners and labourers in hard rock mining.

Wells was a mining company town named after Fred Wells, a gold prospector and a director of Cariboo Gold Quartz Mines. He discovered quartz rock with gold-rich veins in Cow Mountain around the Barkerville area near the Jack of Clubs Lake in 1927. But successful production did not begin until 1933 when the first gold brick was shipped out of the Cariboo.

This second round of the Cariboo gold rush was lode mining; it required teamwork to extract the gold from tunnels in the mountain. The mining companies offered a wage of five dollars a day. When such news reached the farmers in Saskatchewan, they needed no further convincing. Many of them packed up their families and drove a thousand miles west to Wells, B.C., to find employment. The company town with a population of 700 suddenly swelled to thousands.

The sudden influx of people brought some respite for the Quesnel business community because of the increased demand for supplies and food. While the demand was minimal, it kept the business community afloat for a while. The Depression made the search for employment so desperate that the Nugget Hotel fed many of the families and individuals without ever receiving payment.

At that time, with fifty cents in your pocket, you could order a T-bone steak dinner with freshly made soup, potatoes and fresh vegetables, plus cinnamon rolls and homemade pie for dessert, beverage included. The sad part of the story is that nobody had fifty cents in their pockets in those days. Apart from bartering to meet their basic needs, not many people could afford to buy any other merchandise. During these lean years, Chew Keen tried to do whatever he could to hold onto the company that his father helped establish sixty years before.

Childhood during the Depression

The Keen children grew up in the thick of the Great Depression. When the Depression rippled to their corner of North Cariboo, Chew Keen kept to himself and made sure his children were well fed and clothed. The children were too young to understand what was going on in the adult world. Perhaps their parents' resourcefulness and the Confucian value of frugality helped reduce the impact on them.

The family maintained its Chinese principle of practicality—food and clothing before anything else. Mon Ho's vegetable garden and chickens provided a good source of food and her skilful sewing ensured her children were kept dressed and warm. By the beginning of the 1930s, all the Keen children were attending the one-room school that had classes from grades one to eight. School kept them busy and occupied.

As the house was so close to the Wah Lee store, Chew Keen often came home to help Mon Ho with the cooking and to share daily meals with his family. He tried to satisfy the taste buds of his family with his creative culinary skills while remaining frugal in his ingredient choices. He cooked for the family so often his children would later recall, "my dad used to cook this" or "my dad did this with that."

Frugality was one of the Confucian virtues in Chinese society and practiced throughout the Keen household. Besides rice, a staple food in a Chinese family, Chew Keen made dishes with dehydrated food from China such as bak choi, oysters, Chinese mushrooms, lotus seeds and bean curd. With some medicinal herb seasonings and a dash of Chinese spices, he would turn the dried food into delicious dishes.

The children's favourite food was *jook*, the Southern Chinese style of rice congee. Chew Keen could turn the plain rice soup into a mouth-watering meal with the addition of pork bones, chicken feet or dried Chinese mushrooms and garnish it with spring onions and ginger. Another regular dish served up on the dinner table was salt-preserved fish shipped from Vancouver or, on occasion, directly from China. A tiny bit of this very salty fish made the plain rice more palatable.

Sometimes Chew Keen brought home fresh salmon caught by the native people who came to exchange fish for flour, sugar or canned foods from the Wah Lee store. The children loved the way their father cooked the fish—steamed with black bean and garlic sauce. If they had more fresh fish than they could use, Chew Keen would preserve it in salt for later days. Cooking rice congee and salt fish was supposedly an economical way of coping with the Depression; instead, the dishes became the children's favourite childhood memories because of their parents' creative cooking.

In the summertime when school was out, Mon Ho would take the children to visit Uncle Wing and his family in Soda Creek, thirty miles south of Quesnel, and spend a week or so on the

Wing family's acreage. Because of the store, Chew Keen seldom accompanied them on these excursions; instead, he would arrange transportation with a good friend of the family, C.S. Poy, who owned a taxi service company in Quesnel. He would drop them off in Soda Creek and pick them up again later. Sometimes the Hoy family would join the Keens.

The children would look forward to the berry-picking season. Under the hot, dry Cariboo sun, wild berries grew in abundance on the hills and in fields just north of Quesnel. There were strawberries in July and blueberries in August. When it was time for picking, Mon Ho handed each child an empty lard can before walking to the field. Often the Hoy family would join them on these outings. With a noisy crowd of nine or ten children, any animals, big or small, would be warned off, especially bears.

The berries were not picked for their own consumption but were sold to the Nugget Café restaurant for fifty cents a can. The berry picking kept the children occupied and provided some extra money for the family.

Later on, the boys found another way to make money—bottle hunting in the alleyways, especially after payday when many men from out of town would come in for a hard night of drinking. The stores, hotels and restaurants would pay one penny for each returned bottle. All the pennies, nickels and dimes made from berry picking and bottle-hunting were put into a family piggy bank. The concept of pocket money or allowance for children did not exist in a Chinese family back then.

There was a movie theatre in town a few doors down the street, but the Keen children seldom went because it cost money. With a little imagination, they found ways to entertain themselves. On hot days, the older girls would go to nearby creeks and dip their toes in the cool water, pretending they were swimming by a pool just like the movie stars on posters.

Sometimes the Keen girls would meet up with the Hoy girls in C.D. Hoy's empty old house. After the Hoys moved to a new big house, the old house became a playhouse for the children. In the old basement, the girls found something far more amusing than toys—old clothes and merchandise tucked away in trunks and boxes. They would ransack the trunks and pull out old garments, hats and all kinds of trinkets. Then the older girls would put on a fashion show, parading in their costumes in front of their younger siblings.

The boys found other ways to amuse themselves, especially Billy and Harry. Close in age, they were like twins, sharing the same group of friends and playing sports together. By the time they started school, they had no problem fitting in because they could speak English like the other kids.

On the first day of school, Billy met Tommy Moffat and they became lifelong friends. Both of them played sports in the athletic clubs. Eighty-five years later, Tommy still had vivid memories of playing marbles with Billy on the school playground. "Once there was a dry patch in the spring," he reminisced, "we made change by cleaning out the other kids. Then the next day we sold the marbles back to the kids. Five marbles for a nickel."

There were many boys named Billy in town but, at 5'2" and 110 pounds, Billy Keen was called Little Billy and known for his natural athletic ability. He was good at any sport he played—softball in the spring, baseball in the summer, basketball in the fall and hockey in the winter. Of all the sports, hockey was the sport Little Billy loved most. The town had only one outdoor ice rink that was mostly used by hockey teams for practice and tournaments. Little Billy and his friends had to find a frozen surface to play their hockey.

Chew Keen never played hockey or any kind of sports. Understanding how much his sons loved hockey, he would turn Mon Ho's thirty-by-sixty-foot vegetable garden into an ice rink in the winter. After the garden season, he would get someone to build a twelve-inch high board around the garden to hold the water. Once the temperature dropped below zero, the Nugget Hotel staff would come to help flood the surface with buckets of water. A chicken wire goalie's net was placed on one end and Little Billy, Harry, Tommy and other local boys would play hockey. The Chinese cooks and staff in their white aprons would come out from the Nugget Hotel to cheer them on.

In 1934, Quesnel built a new rink; Roddis Shield was the rink manager. He organized two midget teams of young hockey players aged twelve to fifteen. Little Billy, Harry and Tommy often played on one of these teams. One was called "Maple Leafs" and the other "Maroons" because the players wore hand-me-down sweaters in either blue or maroon. The only protective hockey equipment was a pair of shin pads, but the boys had great fun playing games against each other.

Unlike their older siblings who tended to have Chinese play-mates, both Billy and Harry were involved in local activities with other boys. Apart from their love of sports, they participated in Boy Scouts and attended Sunday school. The Cub master was Reverend Love of the United Church; the Scoutmaster was Reverend Higgs of the Anglican Church.

One of the Scout badges they had to earn was swimming. The famous "ol' swimming hole" in Quesnel was the boys' hideout. As they remembered, it was a slough created by the Quesnel River near the railway station behind brushes and trees. Only used by the boys. "No thought was given to swimsuits or intruders."

Swimming in the river would have worried their mother. The older son of Wong Ming Chow drowned in the Quesnel River in 1926 while swimming with his friends. But, boys would be boys. When Billy was twelve years old, a stone struck him in the eye while playing in the school playground. With blood dripping from the wound, the doctor first thought Billy would lose sight in that eye, but after examination, it was found that only the eyelid was torn. More frightening was Harry's accident.

The boys used to ride old bicycles that the Wah Lee store used for deliveries. On the day of the accident, eleven-year-old Harry was riding his bicycle with his friend on the street as usual when a car at an intersection suddenly hit him. His right leg sustained a compound complex fracture so serious that Dr. Oliver, a young doctor, suggested amputation. Fortunately, Dr. Baker was present and saved Harry's leg by putting the shattered leg back together using his own method.

For two months, Harry lay in the hospital bed waiting for his bones to heal. Every day his mother went to visit him and brought him homemade food along with his father's special herb medicine to help the healing process. As a result, his right leg was a bit shorter than the left, but he still had both legs to walk and run on. Despite the ordeal, he continued to participate in sports and other activities.

Coming of age

There were seven years between Kin Ying and Harry. When Harry entered his second year of school, Kin Ying had already finished grade eight, her last year of education. In Quesnel, there were not many girls attending high school. Only a couple of white girls went further to university or vocational schools at that time. For the Keen girls, this was not an option.

According to the school report in the town newspaper, Kin Ying was promoted to grade nine, but she was not told, nor did it cross her mind to pursue a higher education. The Keen family followed the old Chinese tradition where a girl's career was to marry and become a mother. Kin Ying was fourteen years old. She stayed home and helped with the housekeeping.

A couple of years later, her younger sister, Kin Boyd, followed in her footsteps.

The first thing both sisters did after completing grade eight was to choose English names for themselves. Throughout their school years, they went by their Chinese names, but noticed that all the other Chinese girls had English names. Mr. Hoy named his girls after the names of the Moffat girls next door. When there were no more Moffat girl names to choose from, he picked names from the moon and the stars. For the Keen girls, their Chinese names might have been a reminder that they were different from the rest. By the end of their school years, the girls felt free and ready to choose their own English names. Kin Ying chose "Beatrice" while Kin Boyd picked "Kay Betty." They came to be known by these names by friends, although to their parents they were still "Ah Ying" and "Ah Boyd" at home.

In the Keen house, there were different expectations for the boys than the girls. The boys were expected to finish high school. Charlie was Mon Ho's oldest son, with five years separating him from his youngest brother. He was quiet and often stayed in the background. His close playmates were Willie Wing and Dan Sing who were of a similar age.

Since he was a young boy, Charlie took on more responsibilities as the eldest boy in the family. When the Depression hit, he was old enough to be aware of what was going on. One thing he remembered was that his parents would send him to the meat market with a nickel to buy bologna for the family. A nickel at that time could buy a big chunk of bologna for the whole family, which would last a while.

He also noticed that his father's business in the store was slow and quiet, so he decided to take a part time job in the Nugget Hotel washing dishes. Whatever wages he earned, he gave to his parents. His father was happy to see that his son had a strong sense of responsibility at such a young age but at the same time, wished his son were not distracted from schoolwork.

When Charlie was in grade ten, he lost interest in school and quit. This took his father by surprise. Chew Keen's other sons in China never let anything interrupt their education, even bandit raids and other social upheavals. Education was highly valued in China and a way to elevate one's social status. In Canada, it was different. A well-educated Chinese could not get a job he was trained for because he was barred from entering any profession.

Chew Keen was wise enough to realize he could not force his son to sit in the classroom while his mind wandered elsewhere. His words to Charlie were "get out into the world and find a job." Obviously, unemployment was a brutal reality in the Depression era. Charlie recognized it and so did his father. There were no jobs for Charlie in the Wah Lee store, not even as a delivery boy. Couie Chow, the chief cook and a partner of the Nugget Hotel, offered Charlie a full-time job working as the hotel laundry agent. Couie Chow was a very kind man and always looked out for Charlie who was only fifteen years old.

Now, Mon Ho had one boy working, two boys in school and two girls at home. Beatrice and Kay were a great help with the housekeeping and gardening. Finally, Mon Ho was able to pass down her sewing skills to her girls. She also kept herself and the girls busy looking after a toddler, June Poy, a daughter of Chew Sip Poy.

June's mother, nicknamed "Topsy," had died of tuberculosis when June was only two or three years old. Mon Ho stepped in to take care of little June when her father was at work. Sometimes Chew Sip Poy's taxi business took him out of town; on these occasions June lived in the Keen household. June fondly remembers Mon Ho singing her to sleep in Sze Yup lullabies and going bottle hunting with Harry in the alleyways.

It was not long before Beatrice reached the age of sweet sixteen. She had become a beautiful young lady. If she were in China, she would have already married or, at the very least, been spoken for. For the Canadian-born Chinese, however, an arranged marriage was no longer popular. The problem was finding a suitable young Chinese man in the corner of North Cariboo who did not share the same family name of Chew. In Chinese society, people who shared the same family name were considered brothers or sisters.

Mixed marriages were out of the question and forbidden at that time in both communities. The Keen girls were not allowed to date white boys; white boys could not marry Chinese girls. With so few suitable males in the Quesnel area, Chew Keen and Mon Ho must have been concerned about the future of their daughters.

Meanwhile, Beatrice was unaware of her parents' concern. No longer in school, she had plenty of time on her hands. At the beginning, she would call on her chums Avaline or Laura, but soon she learned they were not as carefree as schoolgirls. As the oldest child, Avaline was busy either working in her father's store or looking after her younger siblings at home. For Laura, she also stopped going to school after grade eight to help out on the family farm and in the store. To make herself useful, Beatrice would visit Laura in Wells and help out in the Sing grocery store in the summer.

Apart from the farm, Laura's father ran a grocery store in Wells where he sold his farm produce. It was the time when carloads of people arrived from Saskatchewan and the store was very busy. Beatrice was glad to keep Laura company and help with the customers. At night, the girls would retire to the bedroom above the grocery store. During her stay in Wells, Beatrice and Laura were invited to the church fellowship gatherings and mingled with other young people.

A church fellowship gathering in Wells, ca. 1936.
Beatrice Keen, second from the right and Laura Sing, sixth from the left.
(Courtesy of the family)

The summer Beatrice turned seventeen; her chum Avaline invited her on a trip to Vancouver. Avaline's father, C.D. Hoy, took a few days off from work and drove both girls to Vancouver to visit the Pacific National Exhibition. It was Beatrice's first time travelling outside the Cariboo country. She was so excited she did not notice how bumpy the road was or how long it took to get there. Although the stay was short, it was long enough for her to remember that the PNE grounds were so big she hardly had enough time to see it all. She also remembered meeting a couple of young Chinese men in Vancouver Chinatown, but she thought nothing further of them.

The Hoy family was well known throughout British Columbia for their large number of girls. Many eligible Chinese men came to knock at the door of the Hoy's two-storey stucco house. By the end of summer in 1936, Avaline told Beatrice she was engaged to Henry Sing from Powell River.

As the oldest girl in the family, Avaline understood she had to make way for her younger sisters, so she agreed to marry Henry, a man ten years her senior. They got married the following year, and Beatrice was one of the bridesmaids in the wedding party. She was sad to see one of her chums leaving Quesnel, but at the same time she expected her time would come soon.

In the same summer, Beatrice met Kenneth Wong of Nanaimo. Ken, as he was called, was visiting his sister, Gum Chew (金秋) in Quesnel. Gum Chew was married to Chong Lee, a Chinese merchant who owned a general store in Barkerville and a second-hand store in Quesnel. Because Quesnel had a hospital and a large Chinese community than Barkerville, Gum Chew would come to town for the delivery of her baby and stay for the special month after birth. Mon Ho helped Gum Chew and the baby during the month of postnatal care.

After raising five of her own children, Mon Ho had become the wise and helpful woman she had once longed to have when she was pregnant with her first baby. She often lent a helping hand to her friend, Foon Hai, who continued having children until 1937. When Mon Ho made her rounds, she would bring one of her girls along with her. Being the older sister, Beatrice was often the one to accompany her mother. That was how Gum Chew met Beatrice and grew very fond of her.

By design or chance, that day when Ken came to visit his sister and his niece, Mon Ho and Beatrice happened to be there. For Ken, it was love at first sight. For Beatrice, it was hard to tell

---

because she was a very prudent young girl and too shy to react to a strange young man's presence, though she agreed to communicate with Ken by letters. Through the exchange of letters, Beatrice got to know Ken better.

Ken was a very kind, self-educated and hardworking gentleman. Born in Nanaimo and the oldest child of six, when he was twelve years old he left home and travelled to Port Arthur, Ontario, (today's Thunder Bay) to work in a restaurant owned by one of his relatives while supporting himself in school. He also taught himself to read and write Chinese. Before he met Beatrice, he had bought a house of his own and was in the process of acquiring a restaurant in Port Arthur. With strong traditional Chinese values, he saved his own money to build a retirement house in China for his parents. Unfortunately, his parents never had a chance to go back to China to enjoy the house.

On September 28, 1938, Ken returned to Quesnel and married Beatrice. The *Cariboo Observer* reported on the event:

> *Wong – Keen: A wedding of much local interest took place Wednesday at 1 p.m., when Miss Beatrice Keen, elder daughter of Mr. and Mrs. C. Keen, became the bride of Kenneth Wong of Toronto.*
>
> *The ceremony took place in St. Andrew's United Church, which was beautifully decorated with banks of flowers for the occasion. The bridesmaids were Misses Annie Hoy, Eva Wing and Kay Keen, sister of the bride. Mr. Charlie Keen, brother of the bride, supported the bridegroom. Rev. R.J. Love officiated.*
>
> *After the ceremony a reception was held at the home of the bride's parents, where friends met to*

wish them the best of luck. The happy couple left about 4:30 p.m. for Vancouver from which point they will make a two months' honeymoon trip throughout the western United States. They will make their home in Port Arthur, Ont. Where Mr. Wong is owner of a restaurant.

Charlie Keen and Willie Wing accompanied the bridal couple as far as Vancouver.

The wedding party left Quesnel in Willie Wing's Dodge car and got to Nanaimo late at night. Ken's family held a lavish Chinese wedding reception for the new couple. But they did not go to the western United States for their honeymoon as the report said. Instead, they stayed with Ken's parents in Nanaimo for six months before they headed to Port Arthur. The town newspaper, *The Chronicle*, reported that Beatrice was the first Chinese woman to make a home in Port Arthur.

Charlie, one of the groomsmen, looked very grown-up and handsome in his suit. He was very happy to accompany his sister all the way down to Vancouver. At the age of nineteen, it was his first trip out of the Cariboo, an eye-opening experience for him. He must have met other young Chinese of his age on this trip and was for the first time exposed to a bigger Chinese community—Vancouver Chinatown. It gave him some new ideas for his own future.

The saddest person to see Beatrice leave was her sister, Kay. She and Beatrice had grown very close during their time together at home. They went to places together and shared many secrets. Watching Beatrice getting into the Dodge car with her husband, Kay was heartbroken. She was upset and blamed her parents for letting the groom take her sister far away. She promised herself: "I won't let it happen to me. If I have to marry one day, I will choose my own man." She was seventeen years old.

Chew Keen and Mon Ho were happy that their daughter was in good hands, but at the same time they agreed with Kay that Port Arthur was quite far. After the wedding ceremony, Chew Keen handed Beatrice a blue envelope and said, "One day if you want to come home, just follow the map. You will find it." Inside the blue envelope were Beatrice's birth certificate, her immigration identification card and a hand-drawn map to Dong Oin Lei. In Chew Keen's mind, his home was Dong Oin Lei, not Quesnel.

Over the years, Beatrice moved from Port Arthur to Northern B.C. and then to Vancouver. She must have discarded a lot of household stuff along the way, but she always kept the blue envelope close to her heart.

The blue envelope containing Grandpa Keen's map,
Beatrice's birth certificate and her immigration I.D. card.
(Courtesy of the family)

A family photo taken at the back porch before the Beatrice's wedding, 1938.
(Sitting): Chew Keen and Mon Ho. (Left to right): Billy, Beatrice, Charlie, Kay and Harry.
(Courtesy of the family)

The Keen family portrait taken in Yucho Chow Studio, Vancouver, 1945.
(Front left to right): Kay, Mon Ho, baby Donna, Chew Keen and Beatrice.
(Back left to right): Harry, Charlie and Billy.
(Courtesy of the family)

TEN
THE WAR ERA (1937–1945)

The hand-drawn map inside Beatrice's blue envelope was part of the Sunning Railway. The moment when her father was drawing the map in 1938, the railway was being dismantled to prevent the advance of the Japanese army in Southern China.

Since July of 1937, a resistance war against the Japanese full-scale invasion of China had been raging for over a year. When the railway was reported to be the target of the Japanese military bombing campaign, Chew Keen knew the war was getting close to his home village, but never did he expect the railway would be taken out all together. In fact, the rails, cars and locomotives were eventually shipped to another province while the rail logs were sold to the locals.

In China this war was called the War of Resistance Against Japan. In the West, it was known as the Second Sino-Japanese War. The first one was fought over the control of Korea in 1894; this time, the Chinese fought the Japanese to defend their homeland. When the war started, no one expected it would last eight years with casualties in the millions. No family could escape from the suffering and devastation of this total war. After the Japanese attack on Pearl Harbor in 1941, the war eventually became part of World War II.

Second Sino-Japanese War

Japanese military aggression towards China started on the heels of the Great Depression in 1931. The Japanese army first invaded Northeast China and set up a puppet state called Manchukuo when China was embroiled in its internal conflict between the Kuomintang government and the Chinese Communist Party. Taking advantage of the government's soft approach towards its occupation and encroachment, Japan gradually took over the whole north of China. On July 7, 1937, an exchange of gunfire between Chinese and Japanese troops on the Marco Polo Bridge near Peking ignited the Second Sino-Japanese War, which escalated into a full-scale invasion of China.

After major cities such as Peking, Shanghai and Nanking fell into the hands of Japanese forces, all Chinese in and out of China united to rally behind the Chinese troops to defend their homeland and resist the Japanese invaders. In Canada, Chinese residents raised money to assist the refugees and help the Chinese armies purchase weapons and airplanes. China's predicament was reported in both Chinese and English newspapers. On August 24, 1937, one of the headlines in the *Cariboo Observer* read, "Chinese Residents Send Money Home." Meanwhile, the Battle of Shanghai raged on.

> *A committee consisting of Pat Low, C.D. Hoy, Stanley Chinn and C. Keen started this week to raise funds to assist in the defense of their homeland from the invading Japanese army in the Shanghai sector. They have set their objective as $1,000 for Quesnel, Wells and Barkerville, and at last reports that objective has nearly been reached. The committee expects that by next week the fund will be completed.*

This campaign is Canada-wide, Vancouver's Chinese residents having already donated over $45,000. In other parts of the world Chinese nationals are rushing to the aid of their motherland, and one Chinese merchant of Singapore is reported to have donated a cool half million. The committee explained to the reporter that the idea of the fund was not so much to collect money as to assure the Chinese Government that its nationals were solidly behind it in its attempt to expel the invaders.

When the Chinese New Year approached in 1938, the locals in Quesnel learned there were no Chinese firecrackers for the celebration that year; a note was published in the local newspaper on February 1:

Our Chinese residents' New Year arrived during the week, but in Quesnel there were no celebrations. All the money that can be raised, it was decided, should be devoted to the war fund and the fund for the relief of refugees and war victims.

During the Chinese New Year, on February 8, another headline "AN APPEAL" was in the front page of the *Cariboo Observer*:

Quesnel's Chinese residents are asking for aid for their stricken countrymen this week. They do not ask that you, as Canadian subjects, contribute to the Chinese war fund, but they do ask that you do all in your power to assist in giving aid to those who have suffered beyond description from the terrifying air bombardments Japan has made upon Chinese civilians. Thousands upon thousands are homeless, wounded and suffering from

the lack of proper medical attention – thousands
of small children and women are dying because
they have been unable to obtain medical attention
or supplies.

White cotton or linen bandages are needed –
old sheets and pillow slips may be used for this
purpose. If not torn up into bandages, hand them
in as they are. Clothing, old or new, is another
pressing need. Medical supplies of all kinds are
needed urgently. For this purpose contribute what
you can in cash. It will be appreciated.

Quesnel's Chinese colony has contributed most
liberally to all local funds in the past – the hospi-
tal and athletics in particular. Now in their dark
hour they appeal to you. Will you pass them by?

The Canadian Red Cross Society is sponsoring
a similar campaign throughout Canada where
there are branches of that organization. Make
up your bundle and leave it at the Wah Lee & Co.
store, Barlow Ave.

The death toll of Chinese troops and civilians was in hundreds and thousands every day. The battlefield started first in the north of China and then moved southward and along the Chinese coast. The anxiety and worry increased among Quesnel's Chinese residents after hearing of the landing of Japanese troops on the coast of Southern China in the summer of 1938. It was too close to their home region, Sze Yup.

In October, Canton fell into Japanese hands and battles surrounding the provincial city were fiercely fought. One of the battlefronts moved to Kongmoon and Sun-wui town—too close to Dong Oin Lei. Both places were strategically important.

Kongmoon was an important trading port in the Pearl River Delta and Sun-wui town was an ancient walled city with a good defense system. From April to May in 1939, the battles of Kongmoon and Sun-wui were reported daily in the *Chinese Times*. Chew Keen must have been glued to the newspaper, trying to map out the affected area.

Newspapers did not provide many details and the brief news caused more worries than comfort. After the fall of Canton, it was worse because the news did not come directly from China anymore but indirectly from Hong Kong. Communication with the village was totally cut off. Any family news would have to come from Chew Keen's oldest son, Lung Gong, which was few and far between.

Before the war, Lung Gong was working in Hong Kong. When Japanese warplanes started dropping bombs indiscriminately in the Pearl River Delta, his family and his mother, Yu Shee, escaped to join him. Thousands of Chinese refugees fled to the tiny British colony. The newspaper reported that eighty per cent of the population in Hong Kong by the end of 1938 were refugees from China. The Hong Kong governor had to order extra shipments of food and supplies from nearby Philippines and Malaysia for the sudden influx of Chinese refugees.

Chew Keen's other sons, Lung Shong and Lung Jet, remained in China. Lung Jet, Chew Keen's third son from his first wife, was seldom mentioned in the family correspondence. The lack of information about him was due to the sudden death of his whole family. According to the village source, he was married with a child; but later his young family was wiped out by an illness. Local newspapers reported cholera outbreaks in Sun-wui County in the 1930s and 1940s. As the villagers in Dong Oin Lei depended on the water from the Tim Gum Creek, waterborne diseases were easily spread by the waterway, especially in wartime. Lung Jet's family could have died from such cholera outbreaks. However, what he left behind were a couple of photos of him as a youngster that he sent to his father in Canada.

When the Japanese aerial bombing campaign began in South China, many people were evacuated from the crowded urban centres to the countryside or their home villages. Country folks such as Lung Shong, Chew Keen's second son from his second wife, had nowhere to go but stayed in the village with his mother, Yip Shee, and his wife who was pregnant with their first child. The baby was born in 1940 amid fear and violence.

Under Japanese occupation, the Chinese resistance force went underground and organized itself in guerrilla-style warfare. Tim Gum village became a resistance organization base. In retaliation, the Japanese army carried out raids and assaults on Tim Gum village and Dong Oin Lei many times. In one of the raids, the Japanese soldiers set Dong Oin Lei ablaze. Wah Lee's house was one of the houses that were burned down.

"Everyone scrambled to go into hiding," Ah Poh, Lung Shong's wife, recalled, "My mother-in-law held onto my arm and my husband carried the baby. We tried to reach the graveyard. We crouched behind a dirt mound covered with tall grass and bushes. For a long time we dared not move or make any noise. We could hear the awful gunshots and explosions. Every loud noise made me jump. Oh, that terrible noise. We were all so terrified that we spent a few days in the graveyard, long after the Japanese soldiers had left the village."

When Lung Shong and his family returned to Dong Oin Lei, their home was completely destroyed; the family living quarter was burned through the roof except for the brick walls. All the rosewood furniture and the beds were turned into ashes. The foyer also sustained minor fire damage. The only part of the house that survived was the kitchen.

Lung Shong fixed the foyer and turned it into a living space. Four of them, Yip Shee, Lung Shong, Ah Poh and the baby boy, cramped together in a roughly nine-by-ten-foot space. Sometime later, Lung Shong was taken away by the Japanese soldiers and forced to be a coolie for the Japanese army; the locals called it *jui zai bing* 'piglet soldier' (猪仔兵). His mother, wife and baby son were left behind to fend for themselves. All this information was unknown to Chew Keen until the end of the war.

The phrase *zouh yup pon zi* or 'fleeing from the Japanese' is how Sze Yup people remember the war. Many villagers organized their own evacuation in the event of a Japanese attack. Some villagers would ask a teacher or someone with education to write down on a piece of cloth - the child's name, birthday, village and parents' names. Then, the child's mother would sew the cloth onto the child's shirt. They hoped that the identification would help children who got lost amid the chaos to find their way home. Or worst, it would direct others to notify the parents the fate of their child. Sometimes the evacuation was organized but many times it happened without warning.

Second World War

As the Japanese military carried out its onslaught from the north to the south of China, the Chinese government hoped to rally more support from the western powers. But western attention at that time was focused on Europe, especially the rise of Nazi Germany. After the German army invaded Poland on September 1, 1939, Canada joined its Allies and declared war on Germany on September 10, a week after Britain's declaration. Once again, Canada entered another world war, twenty years after the Great War, and the Canadian government began enlisting young men to serve their country. In the village of Quesnel and vicinity, at least two hundred fifty young people were called up for service throughout the war. Everything was geared up for the war effort.

On December 2, 1939, in a corner of the *Cariboo Observer*, a headline read:

QUESNEL'S OLDEST BUSINESS
CLOSES DOORS

Wah Lee Company, which is one of the few remaining links with the pioneer days of the Cariboo, and which has been in business here for close to seventy years, closed its doors last week. The property, fixtures and stock will be sold shortly.

Wah Lee & Co. had suffered throughout the Great Depression. The Sino-Japanese War dealt a heavy blow to the company's business and pushed it to the verge of collapse. When Canada entered World War II, it was the final blow. By year's end, Wah Lee & Co. was gone; everything was auctioned off. The decision to close the company must have been hard for sixty-three-year-old Chew Keen; he had worked in the company for over forty years, since 1895.

With the company gone, Chew Keen and his family remained in Quesnel. He was free from daily business duties for the first time in his life, but not free from worries of his family in China or his family responsibilities. Though five of his nine children were married and one was working, Chew Keen still had three children at home—Kay, Billy and Harry.

After going through the Great Depression, the young Keens had matured and were striving for their independence, especially Kay. She grew into a spirited and outgoing young woman. After her sister left for Port Arthur, Kay spent a lot of her time with the Hoy girls, helping out in the Hoy store. She also travelled to Wells to visit her cousins, Lorna and Eva Wing. In 1938, her uncle, C.S. Wing, moved his family from Soda Creek to Wells, where the quarry's gold-mining production was kicking into high gear. The economy appeared to be on the track of recovery from the Depression.

Kay was approaching her twentieth birthday and there was no prospect of a suitor in sight. That would have been a concern of her parents, but not Kay. She refused to go down the traditional Chinese marriage path, in which girls did not have much to say. Besides, there was so much going on in the world – the loss of the family business, the Sino-Japanese War and the outbreak of the Second World War. Finding a husband was the least of her concern.

When Canada entered the war, Kay and the older Hoy girls, May, Anne and Yvonne answered the call of the Red Cross by voluntarily registering with the organization in Quesnel. "We cannot fight, but we can help" the Red Cross slogan read, imploring Canadian women from ages sixteen to sixty-five to register. They took a nursing course organized by the Red Cross in case they were called on to help.

Little Billy, then a good and serious hockey player, had one more year to go before his high school graduation. He played in a junior hockey team named the Millionaires. After many of the senior team players were called to service, the town hockey club was going to call off the hockey season for the year. But the junior team decided to step up to the plate, keeping the community's spirits up during wartime. The junior Millionaires were so good and entertaining they captured the championship of North Cariboo for two seasons.

Billy, in his No. 8 hockey jersey, with his Junior Millionaires teammates, ca. 1941.
(Courtesy of the family)

After high school graduation, many of the team players were called up for military services, except Little Billy. Sitting on the sidelines, he watched his teammates Wade, Moffat, Lebourdais, Tingley, Marsh, Boyd and Hill go for military training. Billy's best friend, Tommy Moffat, later joined the Royal Air Force.

It was very clear why Little Billy was not called—he was Chinese. At the time, Canadian-born Chinese were banned from joining the Canadian Armed Forces. Frustrated and demoralized, Little Billy left Quesnel by bus in early July of 1941. He was headed for Vancouver en route to Port Arthur, where he was going to work in his brother-in-law's restaurant.

Harry, a happy-go-lucky boy, was sad to see his brother leave. He was only sixteen years old and in his second year of high school. Despite his injured leg, he was not deterred from participating in any sport. He took an interest in sport reporting for the local newspaper and went along with sport teams. Since the age of fifteen, he held a part-time job delivering the *Vancouver Province* and *Star Weekly* newspapers. Along with his school-work, sports and part-time job, he never gave up his long-time involvement with the Boy Scouts. He became one of five King Scouts in January 1941. That same year, Harry went to his first school dance.

As the war progressed, rumours began to spread about hiring Chinese in Vancouver shipyards. That was the first time that the Chinese immigrants would be employed by Canadian companies for the work that required some professional skills. To be an engineer, nurse or teacher used to be all but pipe dreams for Canadian-born Chinese. But with so many Canadian men being called to the armed forces, shipyards in Vancouver needed workers to fill the vacancies. They began to hire Chinese labourers.

This news piqued Charlie's interest. He had been working in Bill Hong's mining company in Stanley for a couple of years and saw it as a good opportunity to get a job with some skills. He began talking about going to Vancouver to get a job in a shipyard and waited for any opportunity that would come up.

A few months after Billy's departure for Port Arthur, Mon Ho decided to make a trip to Ontario. She missed her daughter Beatrice whom she had not seen for a few years since the wedding. Now that Billy had joined his sister, Mon Ho wanted to see how her children were doing in their new place. It was her first time travelling outside the Cariboo region since her arrival in Canada twenty-five years earlier by stagecoach. Mon Ho took Kay along with her as her travel companion and interpreter.

Until then, Kay had never travelled outside the Cariboo. This too was her first trip; she must have been very excited in anticipation of seeing her sister again. It was a long train ride. They first took the Pacific Great Eastern Railway to North Vancouver and then transferred onto the Canadian Pacific Railway to Port Arthur. They left for the trip in November 1941, unaware that the war situation would soon change.

On December 7, Japan attacked the U.S. naval base in Pearl Harbor. The following day, Japan invaded Hong Kong and occupied the British colony. Britain and Canada declared war on Japan, and in this context Canada also considered Japanese Canadians as enemy aliens. The Canadian government swiftly removed Japanese Canadians from their homes and relocated them one hundred miles from the coast or sent them to internment camps. Their properties, businesses and personal possessions were confiscated and sold at very low prices.

The Fall of Hong Kong came as a devastating blow to Chew Keen because it severed his last contact with his family in Hong Kong and China. On June 13, 1942, a news report ran with the headline "Pioneer Chinese Resident Buys Business At Coast."

> *C. Keen, who had been connected with the famous old time Cariboo firm of Wah Lee & Company left on Tuesday's train for Vancouver, where he has purchased a business on Hastings Street.*
>
> *The many friends of Mr. Keen throughout this area will be sorry to see him leave. He was accompanied by his daughter Kay and son Harry; both of them were popular with the younger set. Mrs. Keen left for the coast a couple of weeks ago.*

On the coast

The business Chew Keen bought was a confectionery store on East Hastings Street in old Japantown next to Chinatown in Vancouver. Although he closed Wah Lee & Co., Chew Keen was not ready to retire and lead a life at home. Chinese people were not accustomed to the idea of retirement. To live was to work; this was the mindset of traditional Chinese.

When small businesses near Vancouver Chinatown were put up for sale at a very reasonable price, Chew Keen took the opportunity and moved his family to Vancouver. The store was much smaller than the Wah Lee store but it would give Chew Keen something to do as well as a place for the family to stay.

The Keen's Confectionary store on East Hasting Street, Vancouver, ca. 1945.
(Courtesy of the family)

Keen's Confectionary & Grocery was on the ground level of a two-storey building. The owner of the building leased only the ground floor for the business with living quarters at the back of the store. Many Chinese families in Chinatown adopted similar living situations—a combination of business and home in the same premises.

As soon as they arrived in Vancouver, Charlie took a welding course required for shipbuilding work. Harry, who was just one year shy of receiving his high school diploma, decided to find a full-time job in one of the shipyards. Shipbuilding was a booming industry during the war. Some companies offered wages as high as ten dollars per day. Such a well-paid, skilled job opportunity was rare for Canadian-born Chinese.

After his welding course, Charlie got a job working at Pacific Salvage in North Vancouver on the dry docks. Many shipyards ran three shifts non-stop around the clock. Charlie worked the graveyard shift; he went to work when everyone else was asleep and went to bed when everyone was up. Charlie would take a ferry to North Vancouver to begin his shift every night for the next three-and-a-half years until the end of the war.

Harry also got a shipyard job at North Vancouver Ship Repairs, where he learned all the skills needed to be a boiler-maker. He later joined the Boilermakers' Union. Although Harry succeeded in finding work in Vancouver, one of his goals was to complete his high school education with a diploma, so he enrolled in night school at King Edward High School.

Working full-time and going to school three nights a week was very demanding. The hardest part was when his afternoon shift conflicted with his evening school schedule. He spent his days off catching up on missed lessons. It took him two years to get the required credits for the diploma. In the end, he was proud to achieve his goal just as his father had advised him since he was a child: "Finish what you start with."

Not only the boys found work; Kay also got a sales job working in a Chinese produce store on West 4th Avenue outside Chinatown. That would have been an unconventional idea for her father. He never expected his daughter to work outside of home and earn a living. But times were different. Many Chinese girls in Vancouver Chinatown went to high school and a few even carried on to college. Some of Kay's girlfriends worked either outside of home or in their family business. Kay wished she could get a job in one of the big Canadian department stores. Unfortunately, Chinese Canadian girls were told that their oriental look would frighten Canadian customers away. However, Chew Keen accepted the fact that his youngest daughter was no longer a little girl, but an independent woman with a mind of her own.

By the fall of 1943, Billy moved back from Port Arthur and reunited with the family. He also landed a job in a shipyard. Now, the Keen family was together again, living and working in Vancouver. Coming from the tiny village of Quesnel, a big city like Vancouver would have been something new for the young Keens to explore. In reality, they moved about within Chinatown and their friends were all Chinese.

In Vancouver, which Quesnel residents used to call the coast, the younger Keens became more aware of the barrier between the two societies, Canadian and Chinese. Their Canadian-born Chinese friends seldom mingled with the white people the way Billy and Harry had done in Quesnel. Most Chinese lived in or near Chinatown and seldom ventured to other parts of the city outside the Chinese "ghetto", unless they travelled in a group.

The Pantages Theatre was the nearest movie theatre to Chinatown and would have made an ideal spot for the young people to hang out. However, many young Canadian-born Chinese disliked going there because of the theatre's discrimination policy; the theatre seats were segregated into white and non-white viewing sections. The view in the non-white section was poor and obscured. The outright discrimination was a new, unpleasant experience for the younger Keens. They missed the friendly feeling of their hometown of Quesnel, even though it was very small and remote. Mostly, they missed their friends.

Fortunately, the Keens were not the only family from the Cariboo living in Vancouver Chinatown. The Wings and Chong Lee's family had moved to the coast about the same time as the

Keens. The Wings bought a business a few doors down from the Keen's store on East Hasting Street. As the Keens, Wings and Lees were related to one another, they carried on the same way they did in the village of Quesnel, visiting each other and getting together to celebrate special occasions.

Most of the time, the young Keens were busy working. When they had time off, they would go out with their friends, many of who were Canadian born Chinese. In summer they had picnics in the parks and in winter they went skating on the city's outdoor rinks. Chew Keen and Mon Ho were glad that their children were busy with their life and friends. Meanwhile, Chew Keen tried to keep himself occupied with the store business, which might be a good distraction from the constant worry of the war and family in China.

By the end of 1943, reports of widespread famine in the Sze Yup region reached Chinatown causing alarm within the Chinese community. Due to crop failure in two consecutive years, many were starving to death. In Kongmoon alone, the death toll was hundreds a day. The situation looked desperate. Chew Keen wished to hear a word, any word, good or bad, from his family in China.

During those dark days, Mon Ho received a piece of good news—Beatrice was expecting her first baby. A month before the baby was due, Mon Ho was already on the train to Port Arthur with Kay. She wanted to be there for her first grandchild and to help Beatrice during her first months of motherhood. Donna May Wong was born on May 3, 1944.

Joining the Forces

In mid-August of 1944, Kay noticed something unusual. Some of her male friends were dropping by her store in army uniform. They came from the war office in Jericho Garrison on 4th Avenue where she worked. Since the war broke out in 1939, a few Chinese-Canadians in other provinces had joined the Canadian Armed Forces, but not in her province. The premier of B.C. resisted the enlistment of Chinese Canadians out of fear that the Chinese would demand the franchise—the right to vote—in exchange for their services. The situation changed when Canada declared war on Japan.

After Japan attacked Pearl Harbor, the Japanese army continued its onslaught on the islands of the Pacific and the colonies of the British, French and Dutch in Southeast Asia. The British suffered heavy casualties in Malaya and Singapore, with hundreds of thousands of men captured and put into Japanese prisoner of war camps. The resistance efforts against the Japanese armies in these occupied territories were sporadic and lacked appropriate weaponry. The British War Office went to the Canadian government with a special request—they wanted to recruit Chinese Canadians to the British Special Forces operating in the Southeast Asian Theatre.

The British War Office was organizing an elite unit called Special Force 136 as part of the Special Operation Executive and the South East Asia Combat under Lord Mountbatten. Chinese Canadians were recruited for clandestine missions in Burma and Malaya where they could speak both Cantonese and English, and blend in with the local residents.

A group of fifteen Canadian-born Chinese had been already secretly recruited and trained in the Commando Bay in the Okanagan Valley by British Major Kandle. They went through basic training in hand-to-hand combat and the use of light weapons. Their tactical training involved how to set up plastic explosives, handle detonators, as well as scout and approach an enemy camp. Parachute training was required in preparation for being dropped behind enemy lines. They were volunteers but willing to die to protect their secret mission. Before the assignment, they would be given two L-pills—suicide pills—in case of capture.

Major Kandle was so impressed by these young Canadian-born Chinese that he urged the Canadian government to recruit more. The Canadian government finally relented and amended the *National Resources Mobilization Act* to allow Chinese Canadians to be called up. In August of 1944, letters of conscription were sent to all Chinese Canadians of service age, requesting them to report to the war office.

All the Keen boys—Charlie, Billy and Harry—got the conscription letter. Charlie was not allowed to leave because a welder on the shipyards was essential to the war effort. Charlie described it as being "frozen" in his post. Harry, due to his injured leg, was not a candidate for army service. Instead, he donated blood to the Red Cross to support the war effort. Billy, no longer "Little," was the one who was able to answer the call. He had been waiting for this moment since his hockey teammates went to war.

When the Chinese Canadians were called up, a town hall meeting was held in the basement of the Chinese United Church where a heated debate took place. The question was "Should we fight for a country that denies us citizenship?" The Chinese elders did not think their young people should go until they were granted the franchise. In the end, the young men decided to defend their birth country and simultaneously fight for their rightful citizenship.

Walking down the streets in their army uniforms and receiving the admiration and respect from the Canadian people, they felt so proud and equal for the first time. Some of the newly enlisted Chinese-Canadian servicemen went to the Pantages Theatre, walked straight to the white-only section and sat in the best seats in the theatre. No one, not even the manager, asked them to move.

Billy, registered as K7614 Private Chew Lung Bew Keen, went to basic training camp in Maple Creek, Saskatchewan. A British army officer, Major Legg, was visiting different training camps to scout for volunteers. One of his questions was "Do you want to go overseas and fight in China?" Billy was one of 125 volunteers to sign up for the Special Forces. They were young, adventurous and intrigued by the nature of the dangerous secret missions they were to carry out. After they were selected out of 600 Chinese-Canadian soldiers, they swore to keep their training and mission secret for 25 years.

Before Billy's overseas departure, Beatrice came all the way from Port Arthur to Vancouver with her baby girl to see her brother off to war. The whole Keen family gathered and had a family portrait taken in a professional studio as a memento, implying it could be their last time together. Chew Keen and Mon Ho knew very well there was no guarantee of Billy's safe return. Nevertheless, they fully supported their son without reservation.

In March of 1945, one hundred twenty-five soldiers of the British Special Force 136 boarded a train to Halifax. From there, they embarked on a ship to Liverpool, England, via Iceland. After disembarking at Liverpool, they stayed in England for a while before sailing to India. Departing from Liverpool, the *S.M.S. Mauretania* carried the Special Forces unit, sailing south along the French and Spanish coastlines, passing the Rock of Gibraltar and entering the Mediterranean Sea. The ship continued its course through the Suez Canal to the Red Sea and into the Indian Ocean. Finally the ship arrived at Bombay, India.

By then, Europe was already celebrating V-E Day, but in the Pacific and Southeast Asia, fierce battles were still being fought. After the long ocean journey, the Chinese-Canadian unit was divided into groups and sent to different training camps, some in India and others in Ceylon (today's Sri Lanka). Billy's group trained in Ceylon. Whether in India or Ceylon, the

Chinese-Canadian soldiers began their acclimatization and serious training alongside the British soldiers.

The tropical climate and relentless heat was hard on the Chinese-Canadians who had grown up in the cold Canadian climate. Malaria and other tropical diseases were another problem facing the young men. Some of them were struck down by the disease and became too sick to get out of bed. For those who remained able, they persevered to complete the training and be ready for the assignment, which could occur anytime, anywhere.

Owing to his athletic ability and Boy Scout training, Billy was well suited to the task. During one of the underwater training sessions, however, he went so deep that the water pressure nearly burst his eardrums. He did not complain and moved on to complete the final training stage of the mission—parachuting. On July 1945, Billy was promoted to Corporal. While he was waiting for his call, news came that the atomic bomb had been dropped over Hiroshima, Japan, on August 6, 1945. Japan surrendered unconditionally. The war was finally over and all their missions were cancelled. The boys were going home.

On January 19, 1946, the *Cariboo Observer* printed this news item on its front page with the headline "Local Burma-India Veteran Home On Queen Elizabeth":

> *Among the many thousands of names of returning men on the Queen Elizabeth when she docked at New York recently was that of Billy Keen, who will arrive shortly in Vancouver.*
>
> *Billy, as far as we can find out, is the only local boy who has served in the India-Burma war theatre. He was attached to a special volunteer paratrooper unit composed of men of all nationalities, and made 44 jumps while on active service.*

This is quite a record, and Billy should have some interesting tales to tell when he again visits Quesnel.

Keen's groceries delivery car, ca, 1950s.
(Courtesy of the Quesnel Museum)

ELEVEN
RETURNING HOME (1945–1966)

Chew Keen and Mon Ho could not be happier that their son was coming home. The war had been long and hard on the overseas Chinese since all communications with their families were cut off for years. Like everyone in Chinatown, Chew Keen was anxiously waiting for any news from his family in China, wondering if they had survived the brutal war.

In Canada, all the Keen children had grown up during the war. Having lived in Vancouver Chinatown, they were aware of opportunities offered in a large Chinese community, but could not ignore the discrimination against the Chinese, which was more open in a big city than in the village of Quesnel. Though the world had changed after the war, the young Keens still faced the aged old issues such as what kind of jobs would be available to young Chinese-Canadian; or where was a better place to live and raise a family. The elder Keens asked a similar question – where to live in their golden years. Chew Keen was approaching his seventies.

After the war

Celebrations took place one after another in the Keen family, even before Billy returned home. The arrival of Beatrice's second child, Gerald Robert Wong, in September 1945, gave Mon Ho an excuse to make another trip to Port Arthur with Kay. Gerald's birth after V-J Day gave his proud father a perfect reason to give his son a Chinese name *Hoi Syun* or 'triumphant' (凱旋). Mon Ho and Kay could not stay very long because they had to be back in Vancouver to prepare for Kay's wedding. Her fiancé was Roy Yip.

They had met each other in Wells in the late 1930s when Roy worked at Chinn's Produce Wholesale Store. At the time, he was a serious high school student while Kay was a carefree girl, too busy with her girlfriends to be interested in boys. After the family moved to Vancouver, Kay became a friend of Roy's sisters, who encouraged their brother in his romantic pursuit of Kay.

Roy just graduated from the University of British Columbia with a science degree in 1942 and pursued a master's degree in aeronautical engineering at the University of Washington in the United States. Kay was then a lively, beautiful twenty-year-old woman with no shortage of admirers in Vancouver Chinatown. In the end, she chose Roy, a very smart yet humble and shy graduate student. Kay kept her own word: "I will choose my own man." Roy and Kay were married on December 15, 1945.

Shortly after Kay's wedding, Charlie celebrated his marriage to Jenny Nann (顏秀真) in the Chinese United Church on April 11, 1946. Charlie met Jenny in Vancouver Chinatown while working in the shipyard. After V-J day, Charlie freed himself from his welding job and decided to return to Quesnel. His brother, Billy, was also thinking about Quesnel after the war.

When the soldiers came back from the war, everyone was looking for work. There were not many job choices for Chinese in Vancouver or elsewhere in Canada apart from being business owners or working for businesses owned by Chinese. The old Wah Lee store in Quesnel seemed to beckon the young Keens.

In their hearts, Quesnel was always their hometown. Having lived and worked in a big city, they felt strongly that Quesnel was a better place to raise a family. After discussing their plan with their father, Charlie left for Quesnel while Billy went through the process of demobilization in Nanaimo.

The Keen family bought back the Wah Lee store building on the corner of Barlow and Reid streets, which had stood idle for the past six years. Renovations began in May of 1946. It must have been an exciting time for Charlie and Billy who were going to carry on the family business under the name of Keen. The brothers had a new plan and vision for the store and they worked very hard to bring the old building back to life.

Watching his two sons setting up the new grocery store and hiring outside help, Chew Keen, a father with a strong sense of Chinese traditional values, pulled Charlie aside and said, "Ah Fee, you're the oldest brother and should watch out for the younger ones. Ah Chick is working on the Island (Queen Charlotte Islands). Why don't you bring him into the business, rather than hiring so many other workers?" Charlie understood what his father meant so he sent for Harry right away. The Keen's Grocery Store opened in the spring of 1947.

Interior of the Keen's Grocery Store, ca. 1950.
(Courtesy of the Quesnel Museum)

The store was on the ground level with the front door facing Barlow Street. It was a retail store with a variety of goods including canned food, fresh fruits and vegetables displayed on shelves alongside the walls. In addition to groceries, there was a menswear section, which was Charlie's specialty. With an eye for men's fashion, Charlie liked to introduce new and trendy styles to the locals. Later he expanded the business to a clothing store called The Keen's Men's & Boys' Shop, a fashion wear store that was in line with those in a big city.

In the basement was Billy's sport equipment repair workshop. Being involved in all kinds of sports since childhood, Billy knew a thing or two about sports equipment. When customers made inquiries about new sport equipment or a spare part, Billy would go out of his way to help them. Starting out as a small workshop in the basement, the business soon outgrew the basement. Billy moved the business to another location and named it "Keen's Sports". Today, the store is located where the Keen House used to be on Reid Street.

The mezzanine in the old Wah Lee store was replaced with a spacious four-bedroom apartment. Charlie and Jenny temporarily shared this apartment with Billy and Harry until they built their own house. The three Keen brothers lived and worked side by side in their beloved native hometown, Quesnel.

The brothers were not the only Keen children who returned to the Cariboo. Their sister Kay also moved back to the region with her husband Roy and settled in Prince George, north of Quesnel. Roy's dream of becoming an aeronautical engineer was crushed. At the border crossing, he was barred from re-entering the United States after immigration officials learned that he worked part time with a student visa. He was not able to finish his master degree and had to return to Canada.

Back in Vancouver, it was impossible for Roy to get a job in his trained profession in Canada because Chinese Canadians were still denied the right to vote in 1946. No company in Canada would hire anyone who was not on the voters' list. Out of desperation, he sent an inquiry to the Chinese government. Unfortunately, China was in the heat of a civil war and Roy's job application was ignored. Instead, Roy took an offer from his uncle, George Chinn, to help manage a grocery store in Wells. Roy and Kay lived in Wells for a short time until a business opportunity opened up in Prince George.

The demand for the right to vote among the Canadian-born Chinese was gaining momentum after the war, especially among the Chinese-Canadian veterans who took on the political fight after the war. They lobbied for the repeal of the *Chinese Immigration Act* of 1923. By serving in the war, their undeniable action of defending democracy and free enterprise gave greater weight to their appeal.

In 1947, the federal government finally granted Chinese Canadians the right to vote in federal elections. On February 23, 1948, Charlie, Billy and Harry cast their vote in the Cariboo by-election for the first time. In 1949 the B.C. government finally granted all Chinese Canadians the right to vote in provincial elections. As a result, not only did Chinese Canadians have the right to vote, so did all Canadians of Asian descents including Korean, Japanese and Indian.

For Chinese immigrants like Chew Keen and Mon Ho, the issue of assimilation was a challenging one. Even though they lived and worked in their adopted land for a long time, they had been marginalized by the government discrimination policy and practice. As Canadians with full citizenship, their children no longer stood on the sidelines. They became active participants and leaders in the community. Charlie was a member of the Quesnel Board of Trade and became a member of the International Lions Club in 1949. Billy lived up to his childhood dream of playing hockey. He played for the Quesnel club, the Kangaroos, and became a local hockey star. And Harry was very much involved in the local athletic clubs and many community projects.

The Keen brothers carried on the legacy of Wah Lee and adopted Chew Keen's good neighbour policy. As the freight train arrived with supplies only twice a month in those days, the business community helped each other out if shortages occurred. Charlie recalled: "The business community was close in those days. There wasn't anything you wouldn't do if a fellow businessman was in trouble and you knew you could help. We had friends, not customers then." With such a guiding spirit, the Keen's grocery business thrived and expanded into different areas.

War-torn family in China

Chew Keen and Mon Ho did not return to Quesnel with their children right away. They remained in Vancouver for a few more years, anxiously waiting to hear from their families in China after the war. Vancouver Chinatown, perhaps, might have been a base for fast, accessible information from China. After communication was re-established with Hong Kong and China, Chew Keen finally learned the extent and devastation of the eight-year Sino-Japanese War. He was shocked and heartbroken by the death of his first wife, Yu Shee.

At the outbreak of war, Yu Shee fled to Hong Kong with her older son, Lung Gong and his family. With so many refugees in the British colony, life was tough but at least safe for the time being. Lung Gong tried to do whatever he could to support the family. In 1940, Lung Gong's third son was born in Hong Kong.

After Japan's occupation of Hong Kong in 1942, life became more unbearable. Trade and commerce collapsed. Massive unemployment befell all sectors. Even with strict rationing of essentials such as rice, oil, salt and sugar, food supplies fell far short for the 1.6 million people in Hong Kong. The Japanese-controlled government began carrying out a repatriation program to deport hundreds of thousands of refugees who were old and unemployed back to the mainland. Yu Shee might have been sent back to her village Dong Oin Lei sometime between 1942 and 1943.

Unknown to Yu Shee, the village she was returning to was empty. The house she used to live in had been burned down and abandoned. After Lung Shong was taken away by Japanese soldiers, his maternal uncle came and evacuated Lung Shong's family to Yip Shee's village.

Yu Shee, whose mobility was hampered by bound feet, was alone and on her own. She could not return to Hong Kong because the Japanese army had blocked all the roads and sea routes out of China. Neither could she contact her son in Hong Kong. She made the foyer her home and tried to make it on her own.

During the year of 1942, the Sze Yup region experienced heavy floods that washed away the crops for the year. The following year, a severe drought hit the region, which compounded the problem from the year before. The price of grain skyrocketed unprecedentedly. Normally, sixty kilograms of rice would cost only ¥50, but when the first failed crops were reported, the price jumped to ¥1400. By the fall of 1943, the same amount of rice cost ¥4000. The *Chinese Times* in Vancouver pointed out that even for the overseas Chinese who were able to send money home, a half-year's worth of earnings could purchase only sixty kilograms of rice. As a result, 40,000 people in Sun-wui County alone perished in the 1943 famine. Yu Shee was one of the victims.

Yu Shee's death was so tragic that Chew Keen could never bring himself to talk about it. He was consoled by the news of his second son's return to the village after the war. Lung Shong had survived the brutal and abusive treatment by the Japanese soldiers. Exhausted but glad to be home with his family again, he decided to move his family to Wah Lee's old mud house in Tim Gum village since the brick house was destroyed. He made a living as a barber and tried to carry on with his life.

After eight years of war from 1937 to 1945, millions of refugees made their way home. Lung Gong and his family left Hong Kong and returned to the mainland. With his friend's help, he found a job in Canton and rented a place on the west side of the city. His sons enrolled in school. Like millions of Chinese who survived the war, Lung Gong could not wait to get on with his normal life again.

The reality was that China had already plunged into another civil war even before World War II officially ended. The two political parties in China with different ideologies—the Chinese National Party and the Chinese Communist Party—were engaged in a deadly battle for control of the country. Overseas Chinese like Chew Keen anxiously watched the civil war unfold for the next four years. It ended when Mao Zedong, the Communist leader, declared the establishment of the People's Republic of China in 1949, the same year Chew Keen decided to retire to Quesnel.

A new China

Chew Keen sold the business in Vancouver and returned to Quesnel with Mon Ho just in time to celebrate the birth of Charlie's first child. A baby girl named Sharon Chew Keen was born in December 1949. She was the second generation of Keens born in Canada, but the first with a full Canadian citizenship.

By then, Chew Keen was seventy-three years old, the same age as his father when Wah Lee planned to retire in China. The old Chinese saying "A fallen leaf returns to its roots" (落叶归

根) describes the feelings of many older overseas Chinese who always regarded themselves as sojourners. No matter where they went and how long they were away, they felt they would return home eventually; even if they could not make it alive, their bones would. Such strong sentiment was demonstrated in the Chinese traditional practice in Barkerville during the gold rush era where bones of the deceased Chinese miners would be exhumed and shipped back to China for final burial.

When Chew Keen first came to Canada, he might have shared the same idea as his father did before him—to retire and enjoy his golden years in China. In one of the letters written to him in the early 1920s, Dah Seen discussed future retirement with Chew Keen and C.S. Wing. He suggested buying houses together in the town of Kongmoon. As time went by, however, the idea of retiring to his home village diminished, not because he did not want to, but because his house was gone and his homeland had become a hostile place for overseas Chinese due to the political upheavals.

After the declaration of the People's Republic of China, most of the Western Bloc countries, including Canada, did not recognize the legitimacy of the Communist government but kept ties with the Republic of China in Taiwan. Without any diplomatic relationship between China and Canada, visiting home villages in Mainland China was not as simple or free as it was before. The outbreak of war on the Korean Peninsula in 1950 made matters worse, for Canada and China were on opposite sides in the Korean War.

Perhaps this would be only a minor inconvenience for travelling. The real trouble was the hostile situation inside China, particularly the land reform in rural China. The reform movement involved expropriating property from landowners and redistributing the land among the poor and middle-class peasantry. Tactics to enforce such policies included holding mass meetings to subject landowners to rounds of criticism or public executions if the landowners resisted or refused the land reform.

At the height of the land movement, headlines in the *Chinese Times* reported the alarming scope of the brutality and horror occurring in the Sze Yup region, including headlines such as "Land reform, no one is allowed to go to Hong Kong" (June 26, 1951), "Two thousand people were executed in Sun-wui" (October 15, 1951), "Twenty thousand landlords and their families were forced to commit suicide or become beggars" (July 3, 1952), "Two returned overseas retirees were killed by Communist Party members" (December 29, 1952).

These headlines were sensational enough to stir up anger and fear among Chinese residents overseas. For Chew Keen, after learning of the tragic death of C.S. Wing's first wife, it was real. Like Chew Keen, C.S. Wing also had two wives. Yip Shee was his second wife living with him in Canada; his first wife lived in China with her two children. Beside the remittance C.S. Wing sent home, his family in China also had income from the rental of family farmland that Sing Cup had purchased a long time ago.

During the land reform movement, the Wing family was classified as landlords. His first wife was forced to hand over the land; otherwise she would have been subjected to a mass trial with a large crowd of onlookers—a form of public humiliation. Feeling immensely fearful and helpless, she took her own life. C.S. Wing may have been spared the pain of learning the tragic news, for he passed away in September 1952 in Canada.

Such stories of suicides and killings came to light many years later. Even the Communist Party leader, Mao Zedong, admitted that at least 800,000 landlords were killed as a result of the land reform. Chew Keen's family in China narrowly escaped such violence because most of the family land had been sold before the war to support the education of his sons. Wah Lee's grand brick house stood in ruins. There was not much land or property they could claim during the land reform.

The disturbing fact was that the Communist Party encouraged the killing of landlords by peasants instead of routing the cases through the court system. The new development in China left Chew Keen with an uneasy feeling. If he were to return to a China under the Communist Party, there was no guarantee of personal safety or livelihood. Mostly, he had no home to return to. Even if Chew Keen rebuilt Wah Lee's house, there was no protection for private property.

Chew Keen's fear was not unfounded. In 1953 Lung Gong informed his father that he and his family had left China again for Hong Kong, perhaps this time for good. He had been back in China after the war in 1945, working in the legal system. As the land reform swept through rural China, a legal and constitutional reform was taking place at the same time. To completely overhaul the legal system, the Communist Party banished all legal practitioners. It replaced the rule of law with the party line and put in its own laws and constitutions instead.

Disillusioned and disappointed with the new government, Lung Gong left for Hong Kong with his family before the border between China and Hong Kong closed. The tumultuous changes in China ended Lung Gong's ambition in his law profession. Another regret for him was his oldest son, Yuk Tang, who stayed behind on the mainland. Yuk Tang had joined the People's Liberation Army (PLA) three years earlier. Given the rapid political developments in China and his older son's escape, Chew Keen had to put off his home visit plans for a while.

Last home visit

In Quesnel, Chew Keen and Mon Ho lived in the apartment above the Keen's Grocery Store and spent their leisure time with family and friends. Chew Keen had given up his water pipe smoking when he was seventy. In retirement, he enjoyed being out and about, following a daily routine of crossing the street to the post office and fetching the mail and newspapers for himself and the store. Sometimes, the route took him a while because he would stop to greet old friends and customers along the way.

Mon Ho, on the other hand, kept busy with her grandchildren – Sharon, then Carolyn and a few more on the way. In 1953, Harry married Mildred May Joek Yipp (葉美祝), a bridesmaid he had met at his cousin Willie Wing's wedding in Victoria. Mildred was born and raised in Victoria, where she attended the Chinese Public School and finished her education in the English public school. In 1954 Harry's first child, Frances, was born.

As a grandmother, Mon Ho looked after her grandchildren as they came along. She would sing the little ones to sleep, not with Sze Yup tune, but a Scottish folk song: "My Bonnie Lies Over the Ocean."

> *My Bonnie lies over the ocean,*
> *My Bonnie lies over the sea,*
> *My Bonnie lies over the ocean,*
> *O bring back my Bonnie to me.*
>
> *Bring back, bring back, O bring back my Bonnie*
> *to me, to me*
> *Bring back, bring back, O bring*
> *back my Bonnie to me. ...*

Her granddaughters, Donna and Sharon, remember well that Granny Keen could sing the whole song in English from the beginning to the end without missing a beat. No one in the family knew where and when she picked up the song as she was still far from proficient in English. Whether or not she understood what the song meant, the tune sounded very similar to a Sze Yup folk tune, full of expressions of wishes and longing.

In June of 1956, Chew Keen celebrated his eightieth birthday in the Nugget Café in Quesnel with over one hundred family members and friends in attendance. He was a very happy man, but in his heart, he had one last wish to fulfill—a final trip to visit his family in China. His friend, C.D. Hoy had made two trips between 1955 and 1956, as the town newspaper reported.

In July 1958, the newspaper speculated: "Mr. and Mrs. Chew Keen are now planning a fall trip to Hong Kong. It will be the first time Mr. Keen has been back to China in over 40 years." In fact, they travelled to Port Arthur to visit their daughter Beatrice and her family instead. However, on July 26, 1959, Chew Keen made an announcement at his eighty-fourth birthday celebration that he and Mon Ho were going to Hong Kong in September.

The upcoming wedding of his grandson Fook Yum in Hong Kong could have been Chew Keen's motivation for the home visit. Fook Yum was Lung Gong's second son and his wedding was the first among Chew Keen's grandchildren. For that reason, Chew Keen did not want to miss it. He also realized this could be his last trip home, so he invited every family member in China for the special occasion—the wedding and the family reunion.

Given that the Great Leap Forward campaign was at its height and there was a widespread famine in China. Chew Keen did not intend to enter the mainland but stayed in the British colony instead. He hoped his family in Dong Oin Lei would be able to come out of China and meet him in Hong Kong. With the tight border control on the China side, any Chinese person required a special permit to exit China before entering Hong Kong. After sending out letters of invitation, Chew Keen had to wait until he arrived in Hong Kong to see if his plea would help his family acquire the special travel permit.

On a cool mid-September day, family members and friends gathered on Pier B of the Canadian Pacific Railway, where Canada Place is today, and waved bon voyage to Chew Keen and Mon Ho who were on board the Orient & Pacific Lines *S.S. Himalaya*, a British ocean cruise ship. They brought two other travel companions with them on this transpacific journey—Mrs. Esther (Chinn) Yip, who was Kay's mother-in-law and Mrs. Chew Loy who was an old friend of the family from Ashcroft.

In the age of air travel, they could have flown to Hong Kong. The only reason for the ocean journey in the 1960s was the enjoyment of tourist travel on a cruise ship. When they first crossed the Pacific decades ago, they might have been passengers cramped in the steerage below deck or in a third-class cabin. This time, they could take in all the luxury the cruise ship could offer in their leisure tourist class. If time permitted, they might have taken a shore excursion at a port of call.

The cruise ship sailed south and called into the ports of San Francisco and Los Angeles before crossing the Pacific to Honolulu, Yokohama and Kobe. Eventually they arrived in Hong Kong's Victoria Harbour on October 8, 1959. They stayed at the Metropark Hotel on Waterloo Road in Kowloon, Hong Kong.

The family reunion in Hong Kong was bittersweet. Chew Keen's second wife, Yip Shee, her grandson and granddaughter, made it out from China with special permits. Later after the family reunion, they decided not to return to Mainland China and remained in Hong Kong. His second son, Lung Shong and his wife, Ah Poh, were not able to make the trip. Ah Poh had just given birth to a baby boy before the family reunion.

Another person missing from the reunion was Yuk Tang, Chew Keen's oldest grandson and Lung Gong's oldest son. Since he joined the PLA, any direct contact with family outside of China was cut off. Only many years later, his daughter, Zhou Wen Li, revealed in her letter to Harry the truth behind the disconnection. Yuk Tang was ordered by his superior to cut ties with his overseas family and relatives or he would be "disciplined." To protect his family, he never told his children of his relatives in Hong Kong and Canada until 1980.

Chew Keen's oldest daughter, Kin Bao, came from Malaysia to see her father. She had not seen him since Chew Keen's last home visit in 1916. Chew Keen's niece, who was one of the hostages in 1918, was also present at the reunion. A three-month stay in Hong Kong was not long enough to catch up on everything that had happened over the past forty-five years. The highlight of the trip was the wedding celebration of Chew Keen's grandson, Fook Yum.

Chew Keen and Mon Ho in Hong Kong, 1960.
(Courtesy of the family)

On February 15, 1960, Chew Keen bid his final farewell to his family in China. They boarded the *S.S. President Wilson* heading for San Francisco. Chew Keen felt at peace for he had kept his promise to see his family in China, even though he was not able to visit his home village. It did not matter anymore if he retired to his home village or to his adopted country, as long as he was happy, for home is where the heart is. Quesnel in British Columbia had been his home for the last sixty-five years.

After returning from Hong Kong, Chew Keen enjoyed his time together with Mon Ho visiting family and friends. His interest in the world and other cultures took him to the Seattle World's Fair in 1962 despite his advanced age of 86. That same year, Fook Yum's daughter was born and Chew Keen became a great-grandfather.

In 1963, Billy, the last bachelor in the Keen family, got married. Billy's wife, Angelina Ling Lee (李德玲) was born in Shanghai and came to Canada in the 1950s. She lived and worked in Vancouver, where she met Billy. To Chew Keen and Mon Ho, they could not be happier that all their children were married and had their own families.

In May of 1966, the town newspaper had this to say: "One of Quesnel's most respected senior citizens, Mr. Chew Lai Keen, celebrated his 90th birthday Sunday. Relatives and friends gathered at Peony Gardens where a Chinese dinner party was arranged honouring the pioneer resident..." Everyone was there to honour him—his children, his grandchildren, his relatives and his friends, even the mayor of Quesnel. Happy and proud, Chew Keen had accomplished his ninety-year-long journey from a country boy of Dong Oin Lei in China to a respected pioneer of North Cariboo in Canada.

Chew Keen, our grandpa, passed away peacefully on September 15, 1966, and was laid to rest in the Chinese section of the Quesnel Municipal Cemetery. His life could not be better summarized than what was written in the *Cariboo Observer*:

> *Chew (Keen) died in 1966 at the age of 90. His wife is still living here and is healthy and spry. She loves life as did Keen and was a partner not only in marriage but in all that life sent her way. ... Perhaps, the store and his loving wife was the gold mountain that Keen was meant to find.*

EPILOGUE

Half a century has gone by since Grandpa Keen passed away. So much has changed in the world, especially in China. The China that was always immersed in wars and political turmoil during Grandpa Keen's lifetime has become a country the world has to reckon with. His adopted homeland, Canada, is today a multicultural society that welcomes people with different ethnic backgrounds and religions. The village of Quesnel has become a city with a population of 10,000 people. His children and grandchildren have carried on the legacy he left behind.

In Quesnel, the Keen family is regarded as one of the early pioneer families that played a role in shaping the business community. As it is stated in the Quesnel history,

> *Wah Lee, one of Quesnel's first merchants, opened his store on Barlow Avenue. He catered to Chinese miners with groceries, herbs, tobacco, clothing, dry goods, hardware, oil, gas, etc. This business has evolved through the years, but Wah Lee's descendants continued to run a store called Keen's Grocery and Men's Wear on the same location in 1947. The Men's & Boys' Wear store was relocated to Reid Street in 1956. After the arrival of supermarket chains in the 1950s, Keen's store phased out their grocery business. Sporting goods were*

*added in 1956 and the family business continues
today as Keen's Sports on Reid Street, where the
Keen house used to be.*

The Keen family has left an indelible mark in the Quesnel community. In 1982 Charlie Keen was appointed as a member of the Judicial Council for the Interior of British Columbia. Billy Keen became "Mr. Hockey" in Quesnel and was presented a lifetime seat in the Quesnel arena in recognition of his dedication and achievement in the sport of hockey. Harry Keen volunteered countless hours in charitable organizations and committees. The Keen family donation to the Community Foundation Fund continues their support for the enrichment of life in the Quesnel community.

From the bank of Tim Gum Creek in Southern China, our forefather, Wah Lee, embarked on his journey across the Pacific to Gold Mountain one hundred fifty years ago. He never imagined Quesnel, a tiny Cariboo outpost on the confluence of the mighty Fraser River and Quesnel River, would one day become the hometown of his descendants. His route continues to cascade with every step of future generations.

CHEW KEEN'S FAMILY DIAGRAM

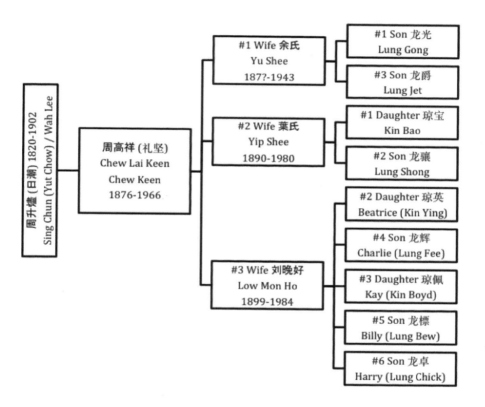

SOURCES

Books in English

Chow, Lily. *Sojourners in the North*. Prince George: Caitlin Press, 1996.

Fairbank, John King, and Merle Goldman. *China: A New History*. 2nd ed. Cambridge: Belknap Press of Harvard University Press, 2006.

Forsythe, Mark, and Greg Dickson. *The Trail of 1858: British Columbia's Gold Rush Past*. Madeira Park: Harbour Publishing, 2007.

Hong, W.M. *And So That's How It Happened: Recollections of Stanley-Barkerville, 1900–1975*. Quesnel: Spartan Printing, 1978.

Hoy Price, Lily. *I Am Full Moon: Stories of a Ninth Daughter*. Victoria: Brindle & Glass Publishing, 2009.

Laut, Agnes C. *The Cariboo Trail: A Chronicle of the Gold-fields of British Columbia*. 1916. Reprint, Victoria: TouchWood Editions, 2013.

Sinn, Elizabeth. *Pacific Crossing: California Gold, Chinese Migration, and the Making of Hong Kong*. Hong Kong: Hong Kong University Press, 2013.

Wright, Richard. *Barkerville and the Cariboo Goldfields*. Victoria: Heritage House Publishing, 2013.

Wright, Richard. *In a Strange Land: A Pictorial Record of the Chinese in Canada, 1788–1923*. Saskatoon: Western Producer Prairie Books, 1988.

Books in Chinese

广东民国史 上下册 / 丁身尊主编. – 广州: 广东人民出版社, 2004.4

广东台山华侨史 / 梅伟强, 关泽锋著. – 北京: 中国华侨出版社, 2010.5

开平碉楼与村落的建筑装饰研究 / 谭金花著. – 北京: 中国华侨出版社, 2013.6 (English title: "A Research on the Ornamentation of Kaiping Diaolou and its Associated Villages")

银信与五邑侨乡社会: 汉英对照 / 刘进, 李文照著; 田在原, 赵寒松译. – 广州: 广东人民出版社, 2011.11 (English title: "Yinxin and the Wuyi Qiaoxiang Society")

References

Chen, Ying-ying. "In the Colonies of T'ang: Historical Archaeology of Chinese Communities in the North Cariboo District, British Columbia (1860s–1940s)." PhD diss., Simon Fraser University, 2007.

Chinn, Stanley. "Finally a Canadian: An Autobiography of Stanley Chinn." Unpublished, 2003.

Collection of letters to Chew Keen (1917–1928). Keen family.

Collection of Keen family memoirs, letters and photographs.

Howard, Frederick P., and George Barnett. "British Columbia Guide and Directory for 1863, Under the Patronage of His Excellency Governor Douglas, B.C. and the Executive of both Colonies." Victoria: 1863.

Keen, Harry. Memoir, draft.

Lai, Chuen-Yan David. "Home Country and Clan Origins of Overseas Chinese in Canada in the Early 1880s." http://ojs.library.ubc.ca/index.php/bcstudies/article/viewFile/839/881.

Marie, Gillian. "Attitudes Towards Chinese Immigrants to British Columbia 1858–1885." MA thesis, Simon Fraser University, 1976.

Old Age Pensioners' Organization Branch #77 (Quesnel, BC). *A Tribute to the Past.* Quesnel: Spartan Printing, 1985.

Wah Lee & Co. Partnership Declaration, B.C. Archives, GR216, Vol. 143-1.

Wong, Beatrice Chew Keen. Interview by author. Richmond, B.C., August 30, 2013.

Newspapers

Cariboo Observer, Quesnel

Chinese Times (大汉公报), Vancouver

The Cariboo Sentinel, Barkerville

Online Sources

Bibliotheca Sinica 2.0. "The Chinese Recorder (1868-1914)." www.univie.ac.at/Geschichte/China-Bibliographie/ blog/2011/12/28/the-chinese-recorder.

Chinese Canadian Historical Society of British Columbia. www.cchsbc.ca.

Chinese Canadian Military Museum Society. "Force 136." www.ccmms.ca.

Chinese Canadian Stories. Chinese Head Tax Searchable Database.

chrp.library.ubc.ca/headtax_search.

Library and Archives Canada. Early Chinese Canadians, 1858–1947.

www.collectionscanada.gc.ca/chinese-canadians/index-e.html.

Rev. J.C. Thomson, M.D. "Historical Landmarks of Macao," *The Chinese Recorder and Missionary Journal,* Vol. XIX, No. 8. Shanghai: Presbyterian Mission Press, 1888.

ia802708.us.archive.org/17/items/chineserecorder19lodwuoft/ chineserecorder19lodwuoft.pdf.

Simon Fraser University–David See-Chai Lam Centre for International Communication. "Chinese Canadian History." www.sfu.ca/chinese-canadian-history/index.html.

The Memory Project. "Chinese Canadian Veterans of the Second World War." www.thememoryproject.com/focus-on/7:chinese-canadian-veterans-of-the-second-world-war.

University of British Columbia. The Chung Collection. www.chung.library.ubc.ca.

University of Victoria. Chinese-Canadian Collection. www.library.uvic.ca/dig/Chinese-Canadian.html.

Vancouver Public Library. Chinese-Canadian Genealogy.

www.vpl.ca/ccg/index.html.

Veterans Affairs Canada. Heroes Remember – Chinese Canadian Veterans.

www.veterans.gc.ca/eng/collections/hr_cdnchinese.

Printed in Canada